SEW
with me

SEW
with me

60 Fun & Easy Projects
to Make Your Own Fabulous
Décor and Accessories

BRANDY NELSON

founder of the blog Gluesticks

PAGE STREET
PUBLISHING CO.

PAGE STREET
PUBLISHING CO.

First published in 2018 by
Page Street Publishing Co.
27 Congress Street, Suite 105
Salem, MA 01970
www.pagestreetpublishing.com

Distributed by Macmillan, sales in Canada by The Canadian Manda Group.

22 21 20 19 18   1 2 3 4 5

ISBN-13: 978-1-62414-631-2

ISBN-10: 1-62414-631-7

Library of Congress Control Number: 2018945177

Cover and book design by Laura Gallant for Page Street Publishing Co.
Photography by Brandy Nelson

Printed and bound in China

FOR DERRICK,
WHO SEEMS TO THINK
THAT I CAN DO JUST
ABOUT ANYTHING.

xxxxxx

CONTENTS

INTRODUCTION

Welcome, creative friend!

Are you learning the basics of sewing with a needle and thread? If so, there are 60 projects in here just for you!

Do you want to work on projects that are a little more advanced, but aren't quite sure how to use a sewing machine? You'll find plenty of projects that combine both hand and machine sewing techniques. These are perfect to work on with an adult as you learn to use a sewing machine.

Or, have you been sewing on your own for a little while and are looking for some simple crafts to make using your sewing machine? Then you've come to the right place!

The projects in this book are divided into three sewing levels, so there is something for everyone! Each sewing project is labeled with the level that is right for you.

- Level 1 is a collection of hand-stitched projects using only a needle and thread. Many of the projects in Level 1 are made out of felt. Felt is inexpensive and very easy to work with. It is sturdy, doesn't fray and comes in many fun colors.

- The projects in Level 2 are designed to be made with a bit of help. These projects combine a bit of hand and machine stitching. For example, if you make the Watermelon Tote (page 97), you will hand stitch the watermelon seeds on the front. You'll also work with an adult to assemble the bag using a sewing machine.

- Level 3 is for those who have a basic knowledge of how to use a sewing machine. Here you'll find simple machine-stitched projects such as pillows, hair scrunchies, an apron and a place mat for your puppy.

Before you begin, be sure to look over the supplies list to make sure that you have everything. Some projects may need a cutting template, so ask an adult to help you copy and resize the template.

Each project will help you strengthen your new sewing skills. Along the way, you may not be sure about how to sew on a button, or you might not remember exactly how to stitch a running stitch, backstitch or whipstitch. If you need help, you can always go to the Basic Hand Stitches on page 10 for a quick tutorial.

I wrote this book with my two daughters in mind. They are learning to sew—just like you! If your first projects don't turn out perfect, guess what? My first sewing projects didn't either! In fact, some of them ended up in the trash, but I learned something from each mistake and that helped me get better and better. Don't be afraid to ask for help. Chances are, if you received this book as a gift, you already know someone who would be willing to sew with you. My grandma helped me make my first projects on a sewing machine more than 25 years ago. We made hair scrunchies and a pillow out of scrap fabric. In honor of her, I thought it only fitting to make sure to include instructions in this book for both of those (pages 45, 51, 55 and 67 [pillows] and 90 [scrunchie]).

The main thing to remember is to HAVE FUN, one stitch at a time!

Brandy

EVERYTHING YOU NEED TO KNOW BEFORE STARTING YOUR FIRST SEWING PROJECT

You might feel a bit uneasy at the thought of threading a needle, cutting out a pattern or using a sewing machine. Don't worry, that's completely normal! This chapter is chock-full of tips and tricks to help you create all of the projects in this book. Be sure to read through the entire chapter to make sure you don't miss anything. You'll be "sew" glad you did!

Before You Sew

Always read all of the instructions completely before beginning a project. Sometimes instructions can be hard to understand or follow. Read them completely and look through the pictures. Things will start to make sense, and before you know it you'll have a great looking project!

How to Use a Cutting Template to Create a Pattern

Copy and enlarge (if necessary) the cutting templates that you will need for each project. You can copy or trace them directly onto copy paper, and use that as a pattern piece.

Make sure that your fabric is flat without any creases. Pin the pattern directly to your fabric. Use plenty of pins to keep everything secured, then cut around the border with your fabric scissors.

If the pattern is really small, you can trace around the pattern piece with a sewing pen before cutting it out.

Marking Your Fabric

You may want to mark your fabric before sewing on details such as eyes or a mouth. Sewing pens are designed with ink that either fades away or washes out. They work well on cotton fabric. You can also use a pencil and draw lightly on your fabric before stitching over it. For fuzzier fabrics such as felt, a ballpoint pen works well, but keep in mind that it will not wash out.

Pinning Fabric

Pins can sometimes be tricky for beginners to use. If you are having a hard time, you can also use sewing clips to hold everything in place.

HAND SEWING ONE STITCH AT A TIME

Threading a Needle

Threading a needle can be tough, but practice makes perfect. You can always ask an older sibling or adult to help you. Every beginner's sewing kit should have a needle threader that will make threading the needle easier. This is especially handy when working with embroidery thread that is thicker.

After threading your needle, tie a knot at the end of the thread before you begin to sew.

Using Embroidery Thread

Many of the projects in this book have embroidery thread in the supply list. Embroidery thread is made up of six pieces of thread that are twisted together. It can be separated into as many strands as you need.

You can use all six strands to really make your stitches stand out, or you can separate your thread into thinner strands by only using two or three. In this book we will ALWAYS use three strands unless it says otherwise.

Basic Hand Stitches

Running stitch: A running stitch is a very basic sewing stitch to connect two pieces of fabric. Poke the needle from the back of the fabric and pull until the knot hits the back of the fabric. Next, poke the needle back down next to where your thread just came up. This will create your first stitch. Bring the needle up again through the fabric and repeat. Try to create stitches that are the same size.

Backstitch: A backstitch is great for outlining details on a project. It is also a very strong stitch. Start by making a single stitch in your fabric, like you would for a running stitch. Bring the needle back through the fabric to start another stitch. Instead of making the stitch forward, poke the needle through the previous hole. Continue bringing the needle out one stitch ahead and going through the hole of the previous stitch. Do your best to make even stitches to create a solid line.

Whipstitch: A whipstitch is used to stitch side seams in layers of fabric. Hold your two pieces of fabric, one on top of the other. Starting at one side, poke the needle through both layers of fabric until the knot hits the back of the fabric. Then circle around and poke through both layers, always starting with the bottom layer. Repeat using even stitches. When you reach the end, poke your needle through your previous stitch and bring the needle through the loop of your string. Pull. Repeat a couple of times to tie it off.

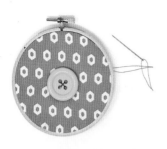

Sewing a Button

Thread a needle with a length of thread or embroidery thread. Tie both ends into a knot. Poke the needle from the back of the fabric and make two small stitches where you want the center of the button to be.

Place the button over the small stitches.

Hold the button in place and poke the needle into the bottom hole through the back of the fabric. Bring the thread across and go diagonally into the top hole. Repeat a few times in those two holes. Then bring through the other bottom hole and go diagonally into the other top hole. Repeat a few times in those two holes. Turn your project over. Make a few small stitches behind the button and trim the thread.

SEAM-INGLY SIMPLE SEWING MACHINE TECHNIQUES

How to Use a Sewing Machine

1. Ask an adult to help you set up your sewing machine, thread the needle and prepare the bobbin.

   Note: The distance from the edge of the fabric to the line of stitches is called a seam allowance. There are many different measurements to use for the seam allowance depending on what you are sewing (⅛ inch [3 mm], ¼ inch [6 mm], ½ inch [13 mm], ⅜ inch [10 mm] or ⅝ inch [15 mm]). Most likely, your sewing machine's needle plate will have a few measurement markings for you to follow. To keep things simple, most of the projects in this book instruct you to line up your fabric with the edge of your pressure foot instead of following the seam guide on the sewing machine.

2. Raise the pressure foot using the pressure foot lever. Raise the needle by turning the handwheel on the side of your machine, and insert your fabric.

3. Line up the edge of the fabric with the edge of the pressure foot on your machine.

4. Lower the pressure foot, then lower the needle into your fabric.

5. Before starting a new seam, sew forward for a few stitches and then sew in reverse for a few stitches. This will keep your stitches from unraveling over time. Most sewing machines have a reverse lever or button that will change the direction of your stitches.

(continued)

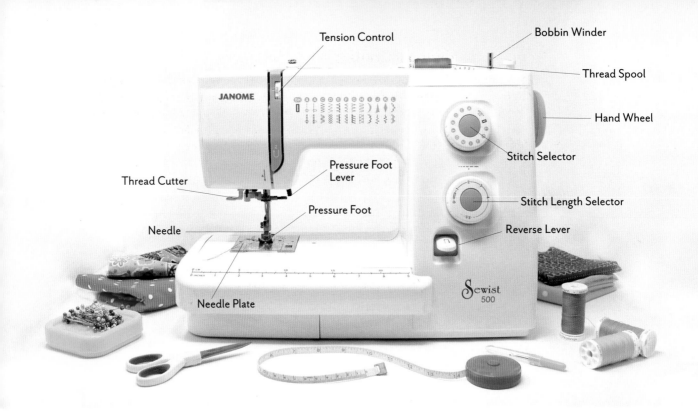

6. Push down on the foot petal to start sewing.

7. Your sewing machine will feed the fabric on its own. Gently guide the fabric through the machine. Never pull it! Make sure that the edge is always lined up with the seam measurement marking that you are using as a guide.

   Note: Sometimes your sewing needle will break, and you will have no idea why. It happens! Just ask someone to help you change it and then continue on with your project!

8. When you've finished sewing a seam, go in reverse for a few stitches.

9. Raise the needle and pressure foot. Gently pull your fabric away from the needle about 5 inches (13 cm).

10. Cut the thread using scissors or the thread cutter on the sewing machine.

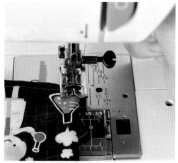

Turning Corners When Sewing

What do you do when you come to the end of the fabric, but need to keep on sewing? You do not need to stop and start your machine or cut the thread when you reach a corner. Simply sew until there is only about ¼ to ½ inch (6 to 13 mm) of fabric left. MAKE SURE that your needle is all the way into your fabric. Raise the pressure foot and rotate the fabric until it lines up with your seam measurement guide on your machine. Lower the pressure foot and continue to sew.

Topstitching

Topstitching reinforces seams and adds a nice finished look to your sewing project. You are basically stitching on top of your project after the project has already been sewn together. To topstitch, stitch close to the edge of your fabric. A ⅛-inch (3-mm) seam allowance works well. You can use a straight stitch or a decorative stitch.

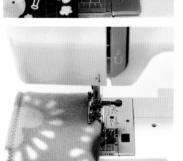

Trimming Corners and Curves

When sewing a project with corners, it is helpful to cut the corner on a diagonal before you turn the fabric right-side out.

Cut close to the seam, without cutting the seam. When you turn your project right-side out, you will have a crisp and pointy corner.

When sewing a project with a curve, it is helpful to cut small slits close to the seam allowance every ½ to 1 inch (13 to 25 mm). Cut slits close to the seam, without cutting the seam. When you turn your project right-side out, you will have a nice smooth curve.

Using a Seam Ripper

Everyone makes mistakes! If you need to take out a few stitches, find the seam ripper in your sewing kit. Stitches done on a sewing machine are super tiny and impossible to take out without some sort of tool. You'll notice that the seam ripper has a sharp, pointy tip. Slip the tip under a stitch and gently pull up to break the stitch. Repeat until you've pulled out as many stitches as you need.

YOUR FIRST SEWING BOX

Before you start your first project, you'll need to make sure that you have all of your supplies and tools ready to go. Here is a basic guide to get you started. You can use a shoe box, small tote or a basket to hold your supplies!

Here are some basic items to include in your sewing box:

- Embroidery thread in a variety of colors
- Thread in a variety of colors
- An assortment of needles in different sizes
- Needle threader
- Scissors for cutting fabric
- All-purpose scissors
- Pins
- Seam ripper

- Measuring tape
- Ruler
- Sewing pen
- Pencil
- Safety pins
- Embroidery hoop
- Buttons

Note: It's a good idea to have a pair of scissors that are used only for fabric. This will keep them in good condition and ready to cut through fabrics of all thicknesses. Keep another pair of inexpensive scissors on hand to use for cutting out patterns and for other tasks.

Here are some more supplies you will need for the projects in this book:

- Pillow stuffing (fiberfill)
- Velcro
- Elastic
- Fabric
- Felt

- Ribbon
- Sewing machine
- Iron
- Ironing board

Now that we've gone over the basics, and your sewing box is stocked, are you ready to make your first project? Remember to take your time, have fun and don't be afraid to ask for help if you need it. Learning to sew is a journey, and you'll learn lots of new techniques along the way. Let's get started!

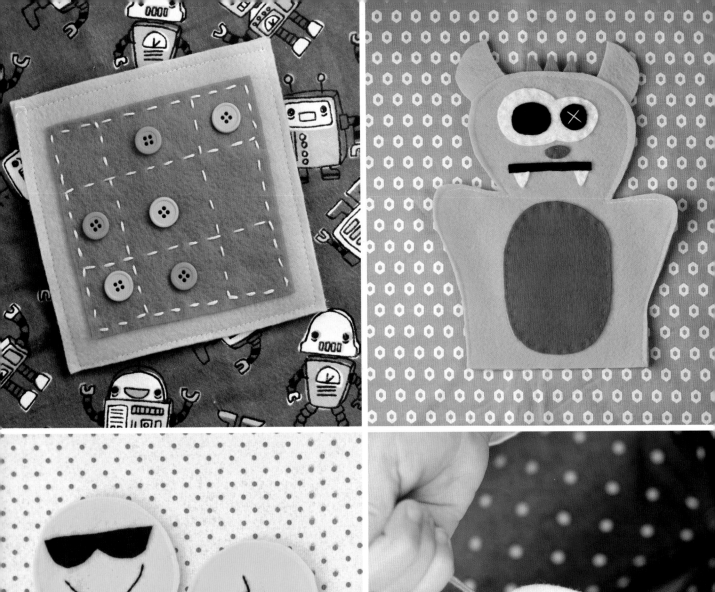

CREATIVE KNICKKNACKS IN A STITCH

×××××

From a Travel Sewing Kit (page 20) to a Hand Towel Travel Caddy (page 35), this chapter is brimming with creative projects that are fun to make and are useful too! If you are brand-new to sewing, try making a Sugar Cookie Pincushion (page 19). You'll create a place to hold your pins for future projects, and you'll also develop your cutting, pinning and hand sewing skills!

A

B

C

D

SUGAR COOKIE PINCUSHION

Now that you're learning to sew, you'll need a place to keep all of your pins. Make a sugar cookie pincushion—with your favorite flavor of frosting and colorful sprinkles!

sewing level: 1

Pincushion templates (page 181)

Scissors

1 (10 x 5-inch [25 x 13-cm]) piece of felt for the cookie

1 (4 x 4-inch [10 x 10-cm]) square of felt for the frosting

Embroidery thread in a variety of colors (6 strands)

Needle

Small handful of pillow stuffing

Pins

1. Using the cutting templates, create your patterns. Use the patterns to cut out 2 cookie shapes and 1 frosting shape out of felt.

2. Cut a length of embroidery thread, and tie a knot at one end. Thread the other end through a needle. Hand stitch the frosting piece to 1 of the cookie pieces using a running stitch. Tie a knot in the back and trim the thread. (Photo A)

3. Now for the fun part: sprinkles! Choose a few of your favorite colors of embroidery thread. For this part of the project, you are going to use all 6 strands of embroidery thread from each length. The thread will be thicker, and you may want to use a needle with a bigger eye or ask an adult to help you thread the needle. Cut long lengths and thread your needle. Stitch sprinkles all over in random places, only tying a knot when you change thread colors.

    The back of your project will look like a mess, but that's okay! You are going to cover that up anyway with the other piece of felt. Just keep stitching until your cookie is nice and colorful. (Photo B)

4. Stitch the second cookie piece to your top cookie and frosting piece using a running stitch and matching thread. Leave a small opening to fill your cookie with the stuffing. (Photo C)

5. Add a small amount of the stuffing, and stitch the opening shut. Tie a knot and trim the thread. (Photo D)

6. Add the pins and you are done!

TRAVEL SEWING KIT

You never know when you might need to make a small sewing repair. Or maybe you want to work on a sewing project while you are traveling! This tiny sewing kit is perfect for bringing with you. It holds scissors, needles, pins, a safety pin and thread.

sewing level: 1

Bird templates (page 183)

Scissors

Felt scraps for the bird, beak and heart

2 (7 x 10-inch [18 x 25-cm]) rectangles of felt

Pins

Embroidery thread (3 strands)

Needle

1 (2½ x 2-inch [6 x 5-cm]) rectangle of felt for small pocket

1 (1 x 6-inch [2.5 x 15-cm]) rectangle of felt for the needle holder

1 (4 x 4-inch [10 x 10-cm]) square of felt for big pocket

1 (10-inch [25-cm]) piece of embroidery thread (6 strands)

2 (10-inch [25-cm]) pieces of ½-inch (13-mm)-wide ribbon

1. Using the cutting templates, create your patterns. Cut out 1 bird, 1 beak and 1 heart for the wing.

2. Fold 1 of the large (7 x 10-inch [18 x 25-cm]) rectangles of felt in half. Place the bird in the center and pin it in place. Open the rectangle so that it lays flat. Tuck the beak under the bird about ¼ inch (6 mm).

3. Cut a long length of embroidery thread, and tie a knot at one end. Thread the other end through a needle. Use a running stitch to stitch around the edge of the bird. Stitch an X for an eye. Stitch the wing onto the center of the bird. Tie a knot on the back, and cut the thread. (Photo A)

4. Change the thread colors, if desired. Use a backstitch to stitch 2 long vertical legs and 2 short horizontal feet. Tie a knot on the back, and cut the thread. Set this rectangle aside.

5. Place the other large rectangle on your work surface. Line up the small pocket ½ inch (13 mm) from the bottom and ½ inch (13 mm) from the left-side edge. Lay the skinny strip of felt next to it, centering it in between the top and bottom edges. Pin it in place. Pin the large pocket to the other side, ½ inch (13 mm) from the bottom and ½ inch (13 mm) from the right-side edge. (Photo B)

6. Thread your needle with the 10-inch (25-cm) piece of embroidery thread. Tie a knot at one end. Push the needle into the felt ½ inch (13 mm) above the small pocket and make a large stitch on the back of the felt, bringing the needle out to the front again. Remove the needle, and tie a knot in the other end of the embroidery thread. (Photo B)

7. Cut a length of embroidery thread, and tie a knot at one end. Thread the other end through a needle. Use a running stitch to stitch around the sides and bottom of each pocket and the top and bottom of the skinny strip. Tie a knot on the back, and cut the thread of each pocket and felt piece before moving on to the next. (Photo B)

8. Place the felt piece with the bird on the work surface with the bird facing the table. Lay 1 piece of 10-inch (25-cm) ribbon on the center of each side, overlapping the edge by ½ inch (13 mm). Lay the other rectangle on top with the pockets facing you. Place a pin on each ribbon, and a few more around the edges to keep everything in place.

9. Cut a long length of embroidery thread (34 inches [86 cm]), and tie a knot at one end. Thread the other end through a needle. Use a running stitch to stitch around the entire edge to attach the 2 rectangles. Tie a knot on the back, and cut the thread. (Photo C)

A

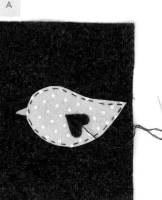

B

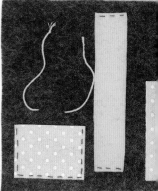

C

E-READER COVER

Make a cover for your e-reader device to keep it protected while you are on the go! This cover will fit a standard 4½ x 7½-inch (11 x 19-cm) e-reader.

sewing level: 3

1 (6½ x 18-inch [16.5 x 46-cm]) rectangle of cotton fabric for main fabric

1 (6½ x 18-inch [16.5 x 46-cm]) rectangle of cotton fabric for lining

1 (4-inch [10-cm]) piece of ⅛-inch (3-mm)-wide elastic braid

Pins

Sewing machine

Coordinating thread

Scissors

Iron

Ironing board

Pencil or sewing pen

1 (¾-inch [19-mm]) button

Embroidery thread

Needle

1. Lay the rectangles of fabric on your work surface with the right sides of the fabric facing each other and all of the edges matched up. Fold the piece of elastic in half. Pin it to the center of the bottom piece of fabric. (Photo A)

2. Pin around the sides and top of the rectangles, leaving the bottom open. Sew around the sides and top, using the pressure foot as a guide. Trim the top corners on a diagonal, being careful not to cut the stitches. This will create nice corners when you turn your e-reader cover right-side out. (Photo B)

3. Turn the cover right-side out. Ask an adult to help you iron the seams flat. Fold the open ends over about ¼ inch (6 mm) and iron flat. Add a couple of pins to keep the opening closed. Sew the bottom opening closed using a ¼-inch (6-mm) seam allowance. Trim the threads. (Photo C)

4. With the elastic loop on top and the lining fabric facing you, fold the bottom edge up 6½ inches (16.5 cm). Measure 4 inches (10 cm) from the bottom, and make a mark in the center of the fabric with a pencil or sewing pen.

5. Center a button on the fabric with the button holes covering the pencil/sewing pen mark. Open the fold of the fabric, and hand stitch the button into place with matching embroidery thread.

6. Fold the bottom edge up 6½ inches (16.5 cm) once again. Pin the sides to keep them in place. Sew around the entire rectangle using a ¼-inch (6-mm) seam allowance. This will close the sides, creating a pocket, and it adds a nice finished edge to the e-reader cover! (Photo D)

7. Slide your e-reader into the pocket, and close it with the button and loop.

NOTE
You can adjust the measurements to make a cover for any device. Here's a good rule of thumb to go by: Measure the width and length of your e-reader. Multiply the width by 1.5 and the length by 2.5 for the dimensions to cut your rectangles. Adjust the bottom fold and button placement as necessary.

STUFFED ANIMAL SLEEPING BAG

Do you have a favorite stuffed animal? Maybe it's a teddy bear that you've had since you were a baby or one that you stuffed yourself at the mall. Make a cozy sleeping bag for your special friend for sleepovers and campouts!

sewing level: 3

1 (11 x 14-inch [28 x 36-cm]) rectangle of fleece

Measuring tape

Pins

Sewing machine

Thread

2 (11 x 20-inch [28 x 51-cm]) rectangles of fleece

Scissors

1. Using the measuring tape as a guide, fold the top edge of the 11 x 14-inch (28 x 36-cm) rectangle toward the backside of the fleece 1 inch (2.5 cm). Add a few pins to keep it in place. (Photo A)

2. Set your sewing machine to a zigzag stitch. A zigzag stitch goes back and forth instead of in a straight line. Sew across the top, using a ⅝-inch (16-mm) seam allowance.

3. Lay 1 of the 11 x 20-inch (28 x 51-cm) rectangles of fleece on your work surface with the right side of the fabric facing you. Place the smaller rectangle with the folded edge on top with the right side of the fabric facing you. Line up the bottom edges. Place the other 11 x 20-inch (28 x 51-cm) rectangle on top with the right side of the fabric facing down. (Photo B)

4. Pin along the sides and the top to sandwich the smaller rectangle of fleece in between the other 2 layers. (Photo C)

5. Zigzag stitch around the sides and top, using the pressure foot on your sewing machine as a guide. Do not sew the bottom edge. Trim the top corners on a diagonal, being careful not to cut your sewing stitches. This will create nice corners when you turn the sleeping bag right-side out.

6. Turn the sleeping bag right-side out, but here's the catch! You want the smaller piece of fleece to have the wrong side of the fabric facing you. This may not seem right, but it is! (Photo D)

7. Pin the bottom edge closed, and zigzag stitch it closed using the pressure foot on your sewing machine as a guide. Trim the threads. As you look at your sleeping bag, you are going to think that you did something wrong. The bottom edge will be raw and the back side of the stitching on the smaller rectangle is facing you. Don't worry! It's right and you are doing exactly what you need to be doing.

8. For the last step, flip the sleeping bag inside out one more time. As you do this, everything will come together, and your sleeping bag will be ready for keeping your special friend cozy.

> **NOTE**
> This stuffed animal sleeping bag will fit your favorite 15- to 16-inch (38- to 41- cm) stuffed animal perfectly.

HAPPY FACE COASTERS

Make a set of happy face coasters to brighten your day! Use these fun coasters to protect surfaces from drips that a glass of water or a cup of hot chocolate might leave behind.

sewing level: 2

makes 1 coaster, with 2 variations

2 (4-inch [10-cm]) circles of felt

Felt scraps for details

Coaster templates (page 177)

Scissors

Pencil or sewing pen

Embroidery thread

Needle

Pins

Sewing machine

Thread

1. You can use a compass, mug or a small bowl to create the 4-inch (10-cm) circles for your coasters.

2. Decide what details you'd like to use: sunglasses, hearts or a tongue. Using the cutting template, create your patterns and then cut them out.

3. Use a pencil or sewing pen to lightly draw a mouth onto one of the circles. This will make it easier to keep everything straight and centered when you sew on these details.

4. Cut a length of embroidery thread, and tie a knot at one end. Thread the needle. Stitch the mouth onto the front of your coaster using a backstitch. If you are making the coaster with stitched eyes, backstitch those to the front of the coaster as well. Tie a knot on the back and trim the thread. (Photo A)

5. Switch thread colors, if necessary, and use a running stitch to sew around the sunglasses, tongue or hearts. Tie a knot on the back and trim the thread.

6. This circle will be the top of your coaster. Pin this circle to another circle that will be the bottom of your coaster. (Photo B)

7. Using a sewing machine, stitch close to the edge of the circle with either a ⅛- or ¼-inch (3- or 6-mm) seam allowance. Go slowly around the turns. Trim the threads. (Photo C)

> **NOTE**
> You can also glue a magnet onto the back of the happy faces and use them to decorate your refrigerator!

TIC-TAC-TOE (TRAVEL EDITION)

If you've ever been bored on a road trip, this game is for you! There is a pocket on the back to store all of the pieces—perfect for traveling.

sewing level: 2

1 (4¼ x 4¼-inch [11 x 11-cm]) square of felt in a contrasting color

1 (5½ x 5½-inch [14 x 14-cm]) square of felt

Pins

Needle

Embroidery thread

Scissors

1 (5½ x 4¼-inch [14 x 11-cm]) rectangle of felt

Sewing machine

Thread

1 (5½ x 2¼-inch [14 x 6-cm]) rectangle of felt

3 adhesive Velcro dots

10 buttons

1. Center the small square of felt onto the large 5½ x 5½-inch (14 x 14-cm) square. Place 2 pins in the center to keep everything in place. Thread a needle with a long piece of embroidery thread. Tie a knot at the end. Using a running stitch, stitch around all 4 sides of the small square. Tie a knot in the thread and cut the thread. (Photo A)

2. Now we are going to create the 9 squares to play tic-tac-toe. Place 2 pins on the top of the square and 2 on the bottom. These will be your sewing guides. Stitch from the top pin to the bottom pin, and use these pins to guide you while you're sewing. If they aren't completely straight, that's okay! Repeat for the other side. (Photo B)

3. After you've sewn 2 lines, turn your square 1 turn to the right. Place 2 pins on the top and 2 pins on the bottom, and stitch 2 more lines. You have now sewn 4 lines and created 9 squares. Tie a knot in the thread and cut. (Photo C)

4. Match the 5½ x 4¼-inch (14 x 11-cm) rectangle to the bottom and side edges on the back of your large square of felt. Place a few pins into the felt to keep everything in place.

5. Machine stitch along the sides and bottom of the square of felt using a ¼-inch (6-mm) seam allowance. When you get to a corner, make sure that the needle is down in the fabric before you lift the pressure foot to turn the fabric. After you turn the fabric, lower the pressure foot again and continue sewing. Trim the threads. (Photo D)

6. Match the edges of the skinny rectangle to the top edge on the back of your large square of felt. Place a few pins into the felt to keep everything in place. (Photo E)

7. Machine stitch across the top of the felt using a ¼-inch (6-mm) seam allowance. Cut the threads.

8. You have now created a pocket with a flap to store your tic-tac-toe pieces. To keep it closed while you travel, add a few adhesive Velcro dots to the back of the flap and on the top edge of the rectangle. Close the flap and press firmly on the Velcro dots for 10 seconds. (Photo F)

9. Fill the pocket with 10 buttons (5 each of two colors).

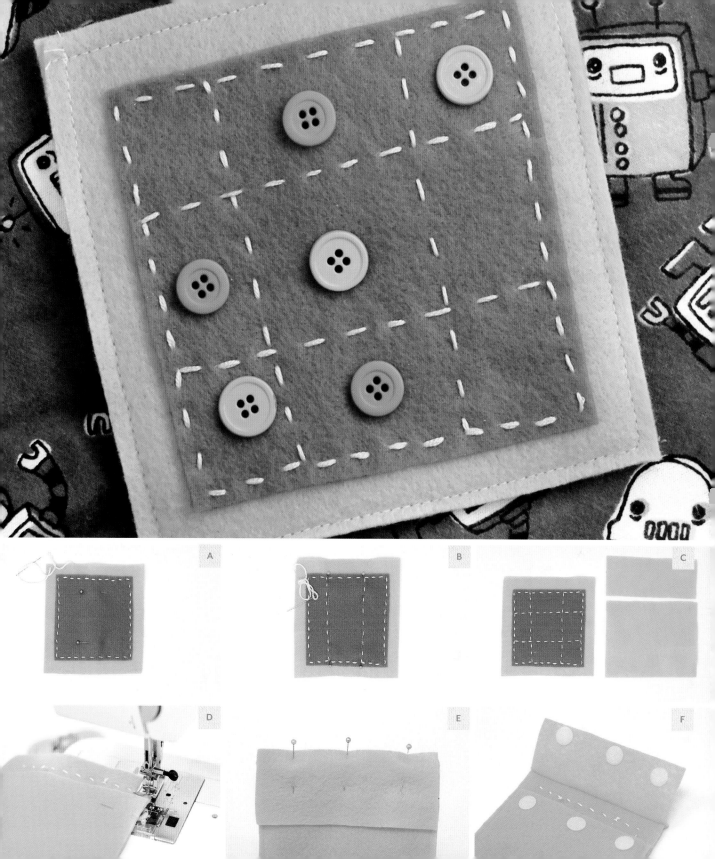

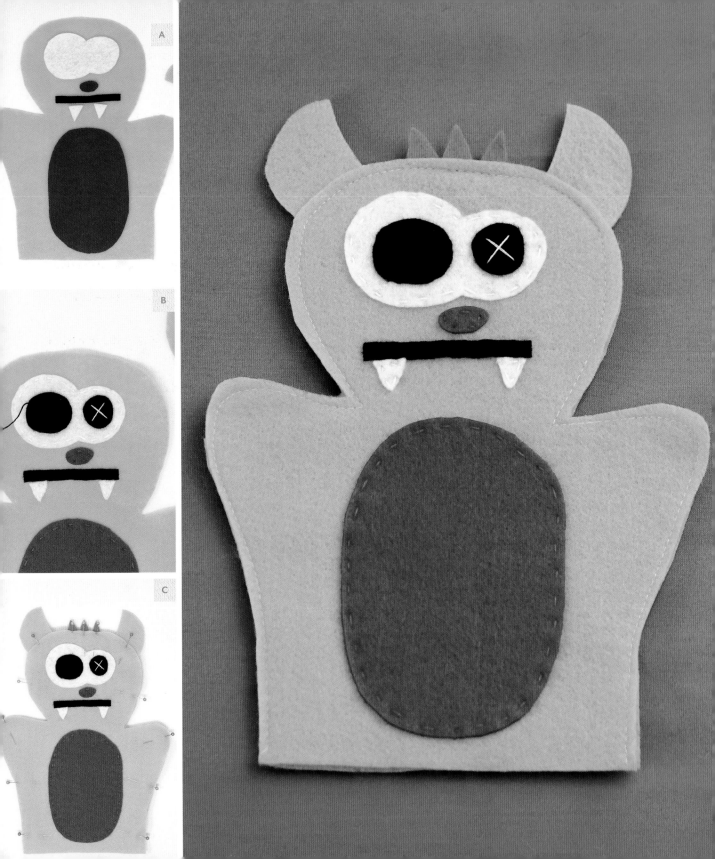

MONSTER PUPPET

This puppet pattern can be used to create ANY kind of puppet, but everyone loves friendly monsters, so let's make one today! Use the templates as a guide, but get creative and feel free to mix things up to create your one-of-a-kind monster puppet.

sewing level: 2

Puppet templates (page 177 and 179)

Scissors

2 (8½ x 11-inch [22 x 28-cm]) sheets of felt for the puppet

Felt scraps in a variety of colors for the puppet details

Needle

Embroidery thread

Pins

Sewing machine

Thread

1. Using the cutting templates, create your patterns. Cut 2 puppet pieces and as many accessory pieces as you'd like. Or design your own! (Photo A)

2. Thread a needle with a length of embroidery thread, and tie a knot at the end.

3. Hand stitch the eyes, nose, mouth, fangs and belly onto the front of your monster using a running stitch. Use pins to keep the pieces in place while you stitch. Change out your thread color as needed. Use white thread to stitch a large X on the smaller eyeball. (Photo B)

4. Place the back puppet-piece on your work surface. Lay the front puppet-piece on top and line up the edges. Pin around the sides.

   If you'd like to add horns or spikes, tuck them in between the 2 puppet pieces. Pin them in place. (Photo C)

5. Machine stitch around the sides and top, leaving the bottom open. Use a ¼-inch (6-mm) seam allowance. Take your time and go slowly around the curves. Adjust the position of the fabric when going around a sharp curve by keeping the needle in the fabric and raising the pressure foot. Pivot the fabric to its new position, lower the pressure foot and continue sewing. Trim the threads.

FUZZY DICE

Do you like to make up your own games? If you do, these fuzzy dice might be handy to have around! This project will help you practice sewing on buttons. Don't worry if you can't get them to line up perfectly. The most important thing is that you have the correct number of buttons on each side! These directions are for one die. If you need a set, just make a second one after you've finished the first!

sewing level: 1

Thread

Scissors

Needle

A variety of small buttons

6 (4-inch [10-cm]) squares of felt

Pins

Handful of pillow stuffing

1. Cut a long length of thread. Thread the needle, then bring the 2 ends of thread together and tie a knot at the end. This will create a double thickness of thread that makes it stronger and is perfect for sewing buttons.

2. Sew buttons onto each of the 6 squares of felt using the photos as a guide. If you have thread to match your button colors, great! If not, white thread works well.

3. We will be referring to the felt squares as "sides" from here on out because they are the sides of your die.

   You will sew 1 button on side 1, 2 buttons on side 2, 3 buttons on side 3, etc., until you have 6 sides.

4. Lay your first 4 sides on a flat surface in order from 1 to 4 with the buttons facing up.

5. Cut a long length of thread, just like you did before, and bring the 2 ends together, tying a knot at the end. Whipstitch the right-hand side of side 1 to the left-hand side of side 2, as shown. Tie a knot on the back, and cut the thread. Then in the same manner, whipstitch side 2 to side 3, and side 3 to side 4. (Photo A)

6. Use pins, as necessary, to hold the squares in place as you sew, and always remember to tie a knot on the end of the thread before beginning to stitch a new side.

7. Lay your strip of 4 squares that you have just stitched on your flat surface and line up sides 5 and 6 as shown. (Photo B)

8. Whipstitch the last 2 squares to the strip that you just made with side 5 to the right of side 2 and side 6 to the left of side 3.

9. Bring side 1 and side 4 together, and whipstitch. (Photo C)

10. Now all you have to do is whipstitch the top and bottom, and it will turn into a die! To do this, whipstitch the remaining sides of side 6 to the sides that they line up with.

11. Turn the die over and add a handful of stuffing through the opening. When it's as fluffy as you want it to be, whipstitch the remaining sides of side 5 to the sides that they line up with. Tie a knot and trim the thread. (Photo D)

Now you are all ready to create a fun game to play with your friends!

A

B

C

D

A   B   C   D

HAND TOWEL TRAVEL CADDY

A caddy made out of a hand towel to hold your toothbrush, toothpaste, floss and anything else you'd like to bring with you the next time you go out of town! Just roll it up and slip the elastic band around it to keep everything secure!

sewing level: 3

1 (16 x 28-inch [41 x 71-cm]) hand towel

Pins

Thread

Sewing machine

Scissors

1 (15-inch [38-cm]) piece of 1-inch (2.5-cm)-wide, fold-over elastic (see note)

1. Lay the hand towel on your work surface with the 16-inch (41-cm) edge on the side and the 28-inch (71-cm) edge on the bottom. Fold the bottom edge up 5 inches (13 cm).

2. You can create your own measurements for the pockets in your caddy or use the following measurements. This version will create 5 pockets: 4 pockets for taller accessories such as a toothbrush, toothpaste and a comb, plus 1 large pocket to tuck accessories such as floss, lip gloss, hair accessories and so on.

   Place 2 pins on each side of the towel edge to create a large pocket. Place 4 pins along the fold 4 inches (10 cm), 10 inches (25 cm), 14 inches (36 cm) and 19 inches (48 cm) from the left edge. Place 4 more pins along the top edge using the same measurements. (Photo A)

3. Using the pressure foot on your sewing machine as a guide, stitch from the fold to the top edge on each side of the caddy to create 1 large pocket. (Photo B)

4. Stitch from the pin on the fold to the matching pin on the top edge for each of the 4 measurements that you marked. Start at the pin on the fold and use the top pin as a guide to help you stitch straight lines. Cut the threads after you sew each line. You should now have 4-inch (10-cm), 6-inch (15-cm), 4-inch (10-cm), 5-inch (13-cm) and 9-inch (23-cm) pockets. (Photo C)

5. Fold the piece of elastic in half and tie a knot in the end. Place your accessories in the caddy, roll up and wrap with the elastic band. (Photo D)

NOTE

Fold-over elastic is a thin elastic used for making stretchy headbands and hair ties. It is available online or at most craft stores, and it comes in a variety of colors.

BUBBLY SOAP POUCH

This bubbly soap pouch keeps the soap from getting slippery in your hands and makes washing up in the shower even easier! Make a spare pouch so that you always have one, even when the other is being washed in the laundry.

sewing level: 3

1 (10-inch [25-cm]) washcloth

Measuring tape

Scissors

Pins

Sewing machine

Walking foot attachment (optional, see note)

Thread

Bar of soap

1. Cut a washcloth into a strip that is 5 inches (13 cm) wide and the length of the washcloth (about 10 inches [25-cm]). Use a measuring tape to help with the following folds.

2. Fold the bottom edge up 3 inches (8 cm). (Photo A)

3. Fold the top edge down until the entire pouch measures 4 inches (10 cm) tall. (Photo B)

4. Now fold the top edge back just a bit, about ½ to 1 inch (13 to 25 mm). Add 2 pins in the center to hold everything in place. (Photo C)

5. Sew the 2 sides closed using the pressure foot on your sewing machine as a guide. It will be a bit bulky as you sew. See note below. (Photo D)

6. Trim the threads. Turn the pouch right-side out so that the seams are hidden inside.

7. Slide a bar of soap into the pouch and adjust the folds until they wrap nicely around the soap.

NOTE
If you have a walking foot attachment for your sewing machine, it may help keep everything lined up as you sew. If you don't have one, don't worry! Just go slowly and adjust the layers if you need to. You've got this!

OH SEW EASY ROOM DÉCOR

xxxxxx

From the décor on your walls to the throw pillows on your bed, your bedroom is the one place where your style can really shine through! In this chapter you'll find organizational projects such as the Flower Wall Pocket (page 60), simple décor projects such as the Bunk Bed Book Caddy (page 63) and cozy projects such as the Pom-Pom Throw (page 64). Get creative and customize each project by changing out the fabric colors to match your personal style!

HAPPY CLOUD HAIR ACCESSORY HOLDER

This happy cloud is just waiting to hang on the wall in your bedroom or bathroom to store hair clips and bows. Cut ribbon lengths to match the size of your hair accessory collection!

sewing level: 1

Cloud template (page 173)

Scissors

1 (8½ x 11-inch [22 x 28-cm]) sheet of white felt

Pencil or sewing pen

Embroidery thread

Needle

1-inch (2.5-cm)-wide ribbon

Pins

1. Using the cutting template, create your pattern. Cut 2 cloud shapes from felt.

2. Draw 2 eyes and a mouth using a pencil or sewing pen onto 1 of the cloud shapes. Cut a length of embroidery thread, and tie a knot at one end. Thread the other end through a needle. Stitch the eyes and mouth using a backstitch. Tie a knot and cut the thread.

3. Poke your needle into the center of the other cloud shape and make a large 1-inch (2.5-cm) stitch. You can use the same thread that you used for the eyes and mouth, or try a different color. It doesn't matter because it will be on the back of your bow holder. (Photo A)

4. Bring the ends of the thread together and tie into a knot. You'll use this loop on the back to hang your cloud. (Photo B)

5. Place the cloud on your work surface. Make sure that the loop is on the back of the cloud. Cut two long pieces of 1-inch (2.5 cm)-wide ribbon. Overlap the ends of the ribbon ½ inch (13 mm) over the cloud's edge.

6. Place the cloud with the face on top, making sure that the edges line up. Pin the clouds together, making sure the pin goes through each ribbon length. (Photo C)

7. Cut a length of embroidery thread, and tie a knot at one end. Thread the other end through a needle. Stitch around the edge of the cloud using a running stitch. Tie a knot in the back, and cut the thread. (Photo D)

NESTING BOXES

These little boxes are the perfect size to hold hair accessories or art supplies. Make one, two or all three! They stack together and take up very little space when not in use.

Note: Refer to the Cutting and Measuring Guide before beginning this project. The square measurement refers to the size of felt to cut out for this project. The corner measurement is a guide for marking the corners later in the project. The basket we will be making together is the 5-inch (13-cm) basket.

sewing level: 2
makes 1 box with 3 size options

1 (10-inch [25-cm]) square of felt for outer fabric

1 (10-inch [25-cm]) square of felt for lining

Scissors

Pins

Sewing machine

Thread

Needle

Pencil or sewing pen

4 buttons

1. To make the middle-size, 5-inch (13-cm) basket, cut 2 squares of felt that are 10 x 10 inches (25 x 25 cm). Make sure to follow the Cutting and Measuring Guide if you'd like to make a larger or smaller basket.

2. Stack the squares, lining up the edges. Add a few pins to keep everything in place.

3. Machine stitch around all 4 sides using the pressure foot on your machine as a guide. Trim the threads. (Photo A)

4. Fold the square in half with the lining felt facing you.

5. Measure 2 inches (5 cm) on the side, and mark it with a pencil or sewing pen. Measure 2 inches (5 cm) on the bottom and mark it as well. Connect the markings with a diagonal line, forming a triangle. Repeat for the other side. Machine stitch along the diagonal lines. (Photo B)

6. Fold the fabric in half in the other direction. Add 2 pins to keep the top corners together. Mark the other 2 bottom corners 2 inches (5 cm) up and 2 inches (5 cm) along the bottom. (Photo C)

7. Machine stitch along the diagonal lines.

8. Cut each corner seam on a diagonal ¼ inch (6 mm) away from the seam. (Photo D)

9. Turn the box right-side out.

10. Fold down each flap and pin in place.

11. Sew a button in the center of each flap (see page 11 for tips). (Photo E)

12. If you make all three sizes, they will nest inside each other for storage! (Photo F)

CUTTING AND MEASURING GUIDE

6-inch (15-cm) basket: 12-inch (31-cm) squares of felt, 2½-inch (6-cm) corners

5-inch (13-cm) basket: 10-inch (25-cm) squares of felt, 2-inch (5-cm) corners

4-inch (10-cm) basket: 8-inch (20-cm) squares of felt, 1½-inch (4-cm) corners

A

B

C

D

MY MASTER-PIECE ART PILLOW

Use fabric as a blank canvas to create a pillow masterpiece! You are the designer for this project. What will you create?

sewing level: 1

1 (8½ x 11-inch [22 x 28-cm]) piece of paper

White cotton fabric

Pencil or sewing pen

Scissors

Fabric markers

Pins

Embroidery thread

Needle

Pillow stuffing

1. Use the 8½ x 11-inch (22 x 28-cm) piece of paper as your cutting template. Place the paper on top of your fabric. Trace around it with a pencil or sewing pen. Cut out 2 rectangles of fabric.

2. Set 1 piece of fabric aside.

3. Draw a picture on the other piece of fabric with the fabric markers. Get creative and try to fill up the entire space with color! (Photo A)

4. Place the 2 rectangles together, with your artwork on top. Add pins all the way around the edge to keep the 2 pieces of fabric together.

5. Cut a length of embroidery thread, and tie a knot at one end. Thread the needle and use a running stitch to stitch around 3 of the sides. You can use white thread or a fun contrasting color that stands out. Remove the pins as you stitch around the sides. (Photo B)

6. Add a couple of handfuls of stuffing to your pillow. (Photo C)

7. Stitch the top closed. Finish with a knot on the back of the pillow and trim the thread. (Photo D)

Voila! Look what you've created!

NINJA BUDDY

Whether you are looking for something to keep your hands warm on a cold day or to cuddle with at night, this ninja buddy is ready to jump into the microwave anytime you need him.

sewing level: 2

Ninja templates (page 177)

Scissors

2 (5 x 6-inch [13 x 15-cm]) pieces of black fleece for the ninja body

1 (4 x 2-inch [10 x 5-cm]) piece of tan felt for the face

1 (5 x ½-inch [13 x 1-cm]) piece of felt for the belt

Felt scraps for the belt ties

Pins

Black embroidery thread

Needle

Pencil or sewing pen

Sewing machine

1 cup (214 g) rice

NOTE
To warm the ninja buddy, have an adult heat your buddy up for 30 seconds at a time until it's just right, and that ninja will stay warm for quite a while! Rice may have a slight odor when heated. This is normal.

1. Using the cutting templates, create your patterns. Cut out 2 tie pieces from whichever color of felt you'd like. Cut out 1 face piece from the tan felt.

2. Pin the belt piece just below the center of 1 of the body pieces. Cut a long length of embroidery thread, and tie a knot at one end. Thread your needle and use a running stitch to stitch all the way around the belt piece. Do not tie a knot or cut the thread just yet.

3. Position the 2 tie pieces by overlapping them a bit on the belt. Bring the needle through the fabric from the back and stitch 1 stitch on the diagonal. Then stitch 1 stitch on the other diagonal to create an X. Go over your X stitches once more. Tie a knot in the back and trim the thread. (Photo A)

4. Using a pencil or sewing pen, lightly draw 2 eyes onto the ninja face. Pin the ninja face onto the center of the black fleece. Tie a knot in your thread and stitch all the way around the face. (Photo B)

5. Bring the thread through the back and continue by stitching on the eyes using a backstitch. Tie a knot and trim the thread. (Photo C)

6. Lay the second ninja body piece on top of the first piece with the right sides of the fabric facing each other. Place pins every couple of inches around the fabric edge to keep the 2 pieces together. Leave a section open on the bottom, and mark that section by placing 2 pins, close together, on each side of the opening. (Photo D)

7. Sew from the edge of 1 side of the opening all the way around to the edge of the other side of the opening using a sewing machine. Use the pressure foot on your sewing machine as a guide (see page 13 for tips on turning corners). Trim the threads.

8. Turn the project right-side out so that the sewing seams are hidden inside. (Photo E)

9. Fill the ninja with the rice.

10. Fold the edges of the opening over and place a couple of pins over it to keep it closed.

11. Normally we would sew the opening closed by hand, but rice is so small and could easily slip through our hand stitches. We need to make sure that the opening is machine stitched closed.

12. Gently shake the ninja bag, with the pinned opening on the top. Make sure that there isn't any rice near the seam. Be careful: If the needle hits any rice, it may cause the needle to break. Sew the opening closed using a ⅛-inch (3-mm) seam allowance. Trim the threads. (Photo F)

A

B

C

FAIRY HOUSE

Make a little fairy house to keep on your bed, or use it as a decoration on your wall! A magical portal from fairyland to your bedroom!

sewing level: 2
makes 1 fairy house

House templates (page 165)

Scissors

2 (5½ x 6-inch [14 x 15-cm]) rectangles of fabric for the house

1 (8 x 10-inch [20 x 25-cm]) rectangle of contrasting fabric for the roof

Felt scraps

Pins

Embroidery thread

Needle

Button

1 (10-inch [25-cm]) piece of pom-pom trim (optional)

Sewing machine

Thread

Pillow stuffing

1. Using the cutting templates, create your patterns. Cut 2 triangles from the piece of contrasting fabric for the roof. Cut out 1 door and 1 window from the felt scraps.

2. Pin the door onto the front of one of the 5½ x 6-inch (14 x 15-cm) house pieces ¼ inch (6 mm) from the bottom edge. Pin the circle window onto the door.

3. Thread a needle with a length of embroidery thread. Tie a knot at the end. Use a running stitch to sew the door to the house front. Tie a knot at the back, and cut the thread. Repeat for the window.

4. Thread a length of embroidery thread through a needle and bring both ends together. Tie a knot. Sew a button on for the doorknob.

5. Thread a length of embroidery thread through a needle, and tie a knot at the end. To make the lines for the window, make 1 long stitch from the bottom of the window to the top, and a second stitch from the right-hand side of the window to the left. Tie a knot on the back, and cut the thread. (Photo A)

6. Pin the pom-pom trim to the top edge on the front of the house, if desired. (Photo B)

7. Machine stitch the pom-pom trim close to the edge. Trim the threads.

8. For the front roof, place 1 of the triangles on top of the trim, with the right sides of the fabric facing each other. Pin in place. (Photo C)

9. For the back roof, place the other triangle on top of the other 5½ x 6-inch (14 x 15-cm) house-piece with the right sides of the fabric facing each other. Pin in place.

10. Machine stitch the roof to the front of the house using a ¼-inch (6-mm) seam allowance. Trim the threads. Repeat for the back of the house.

(continued)

11. Place the back house-piece on the work surface with the right side of the fabric facing up. Lay the front house-piece on top with the right side of the fabric facing down.

12. Place pins along the edge to keep the 2 fabric pieces together. It sometimes helps to place 2 pins on each side of the opening for your stuffing. This will help you remember to stop sewing when you get to the double pins. (Photo D)

13. Start sewing at one set of double pins and continue around your entire house until you reach the second set of double pins. Use your sewing machine pressure foot as a guide, keeping your fabric lined up with it as you sew. When you get to a corner, make sure that the needle is down in the fabric before you lift the pressure foot to turn the fabric. After you turn the fabric, lower the pressure foot again and continue sewing. Trim the threads.

14. After sewing all sides, carefully trim a small triangle off each corner for a finished look when you turn your fairy house right-side out. Make sure not to cut too closely to your seam.

15. Turn the house right-side out through the opening in the fabric. Add a couple of small handfuls of stuffing through the opening.

16. Fold the sides of the opening over to hide unfinished fabric edges. Pin in place.

17. Thread a needle with thread. Tie a knot at the end. Stitch the opening closed with a whipstitch. Tie a knot at the back, and cut the thread. (Photo E)

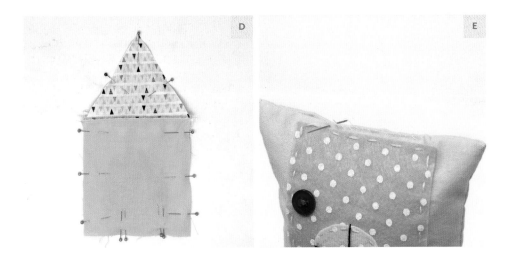

D

E

READING PILLOW

There's nothing like having a good book to read on a rainy day, in the car or before bed! Make a reading pillow to cozy up to the next time you read. It even has a pocket to hold your book!

sewing level: 3

3 (18-inch [46-cm]) squares of flannel fabric

Iron

Ironing board

Pins

Sewing machine

Thread

Scissors

6–8 big handfuls of pillow stuffing

1. You will need 3 squares of fabric: 2 for the pillow and 1 for the pocket. You can make them all the same or use a different fabric for each square.

2. Fold the pocket square in half with the right side of the fabric on the outside. Ask an adult to help you press the fold with an iron so that it is nice and flat.

3. Lay 1 square on your work surface. Make sure the printed side of the fabric is facing you. Lay your pocket piece on top. It should be exactly half the size of your big square. Line up the edges, and make sure that the folded side that you ironed is on the top. (Photo A)

4. Place the second square on top, sandwiching your pocket in between the squares. The wrong side of the fabric should be facing you.

This might not look right to you, but don't worry, it is! When you sew you usually want the pretty side of the fabrics facing each other, and the wrong side of the fabric facing you. After you sew the seam, you will flip it right-side out. That means that the right side of the fabric will be facing you again—and all of your stitches will be hidden!

5. To keep everything together while you sew, place pins every few inches all the way around. Make sure to leave a section open so that you can turn your pillow right-side out after you sew! It sometimes helps to place 2 pins on each side of the opening for your stuffing. This will help you remember to stop sewing when you get to the double pins. (Photo B)

6. Start sewing at one set of double pins and continue around the pillow. Use the sewing machine pressure foot as a guide, keeping your fabric lined up with it as you sew. When you reach a corner, make sure that the needle is in the fabric. Lift the pressure foot, adjust the direction of the fabric and lower the pressure foot once more. Continue to sew until you reach the second set of double pins. Trim the threads.

(continued)

7. After sewing all the sides, carefully trim a small triangle off each corner for a neater finish to the pillow. Make sure not to cut too closely to your seam.

8. Turn the pillow right-side out. (Photo C)

9. No pillow is complete without some stuffing to make it nice and cozy! Grab a few handfuls of stuffing and put it inside the pillow using the opening on the side. Continue stuffing the pillow until it is as firm as you'd like.

10. Fold the sides of the opening over to hide unfinished fabric edges. Pin in place. (Photo D)

11. Cut a 20-inch (51-cm) length of thread. Thread a needle and pull both ends of the thread together and tie a knot. This will create a double thickness of thread and stronger stitches. Stitch the opening closed with a whipstitch. Tie a knot and cut the thread.

12. Slide your favorite book into the pocket and enjoy your new favorite pillow!

TOOTH FAIRY PILLOW

Sometimes it can be hard for the tooth fairy to find a tiny tooth in the dark. Why not help her out by making an adorable little pillow to hold your tooth?

sewing level: 1

Tooth template (page 185)

Scissors

1 (8½ x 11-inch [22 x 28-cm]) sheet of white felt

1 (1½ x 1½-inch [4 x 4-cm]) square of felt for the pocket

Pins

Embroidery thread

Needle

2 small buttons

Pencil or sewing pen

Pillow stuffing (optional)

1. Using the cutting template, create your pattern. Cut out 2 tooth shapes from the white felt.

2. Pin the pocket to the center of 1 of the tooth shapes. This will be the back of your pillow. Cut a long length of embroidery thread, and tie a knot at one end. Thread the other end with a needle. Stitch around the sides and bottom of the pocket using a running stitch. Tie a knot on the back and trim off any extra thread. Set aside. (Photo A)

3. Thread a needle with thread for the button eyes, and tie a knot at one end. Sew 2 button eyes onto the other tooth shape. Tie a knot on the back and trim off any extra thread. This will be the front of your pillow. (Photo B)

4. Lightly draw a mouth onto the front using a pencil or sewing pen.

5. Thread a needle with thread for the mouth. Tie a knot on the end of the thread. Stitch the mouth onto the tooth shape using a backstitch. Tie a knot on the back and trim off any extra thread.

6. Lay the back pillow piece on your work surface. Make sure the pocket is against your work surface. Place the other pillow piece on top with the eyes and mouth facing you. Pin it all the way around to keep the pieces together. If you want your pillow to be a little fluffy, you can add a tiny bit of stuffing before adding the last 3 pins. (Photo C)

7. Cut a long piece of thread. Tie a knot at one end, and thread a needle with the other end. Whipstitch all the way around the tooth. Tie a knot and cut your thread. (Photo D)

FLOWER PENCIL POT

Brighten up your desk with a pot of spring flowers—pencil flowers! This cute pot of flowers would also make a great gift idea for Mother's Day or Teacher Appreciation Day!

sewing level: 1

Flower templates (page 165)

Scissors

Felt scraps

Embroidery thread

Needle

Pencils

Styrofoam ball

Flower pot

1. Using the cutting templates, create your patterns. Cut out 1 flower shape and 1 circle for each flower that you'd like to make.

2. Cut a length of embroidery thread, and tie a knot at one end. Thread the other end through a needle. Center the circle in the middle of the flower and stitch around the edge using a running stitch. Leave an opening on the circle large enough to slide a pencil in. Tie a knot on the back, and cut the thread. (Photo A)

3. Slide each flower over a pencil eraser. (Photo B)

4. Place a Styrofoam ball inside a small flower pot.

5. Push the pencil into the Styrofoam ball to keep it in place. Repeat until you have a beautiful pot of flowers.

COZY PILLOWCASE

Pillowcases are easy to make and so cozy to lay on when you use fleece fabric. You can find fleece in so many colors and patterns!

sewing level: 3

1 (42 x 8-inch [107 x 20-cm]) rectangle of fleece for the border (see note)

Pins

Sewing machine

Thread

1 (42 x 22-inch [107 x 56-cm]) rectangle of fleece for the main piece

Scissors

1. Fold one long edge of the 42 x 8-inch (107 x 20-cm) rectangle over 1 inch (2.5 cm). Place pins along the edge to keep the fold in place.

2. Set your machine stitch to a zigzag stitch for the entire project.

3. Sew across the long edge of the border piece, creating a 1-inch (2.5-cm) hem. (Photo A)

4. With the right sides of the fabric facing each other, pin the border piece to one of the long edges on the 42 x 22-inch (107 x 56-cm) piece. Sew the pieces together using the pressure foot on your sewing machine as a guide.

5. You will now have a giant rectangle of fabric with the main fabric on the top and the border piece on the bottom. Fold this piece in half width-wise with the right sides of the fabric touching.

6. Pin along the top and the side. (Photo B)

7. Sew along the top and the side, using the pressure foot as a guide, and removing the pins as you go. Carefully cut the top corners on a diagonal, but do not cut your stitching. This will make the corners nice and pointy when you turn your project right-side out. (Photo C)

8. Turn your new pillowcase right-side out and fill with a standard-size pillow!

NOTE

Fleece fabric is stretchy. Give it a little tug and see for yourself! When cutting out your rectangles, make sure that the stretch is going from side to side, and not up and down. If you aren't sure if your fleece is facing the right direction, ask an adult to double-check it with you!

FLOWER WALL POCKET

A wall pocket is the perfect place to hold letters, birthday cards or other keepsakes. Hang it on the back of a door or over your desk!

sewing level: 1

1 (8½ x 11-inch [22 x 28-cm]) piece of copy paper

Ruler

Pencil or pen

Scissors

1 (8½ x 11-inch [22 x 28-cm]) piece of felt for the main piece

Flower templates (page 163)

1 (4 x 4-inch [10 x 10-cm]) square of felt for the flower

1 (8 x 2-inch [20 x 5-cm]) rectangle of felt for the flower leaves

Pins

Needle

Embroidery thread

1 (6 x 5-inch [15 x 13-cm]) rectangle for the pocket

Large button

1 (10–12-inch [25–31-cm]) piece of ¼-inch (6-mm) dowel

1. Fold the copy paper in half with the fold on the left. Use a ruler and pen to make a mark 2 inches (5 cm) from the bottom right edge. Line up the straight edge of the ruler with the mark and the bottom left corner of the paper. Draw a line connecting the 2 points. (Photo A)

2. Cut on the line. Open the paper on the fold and use this as a template for the main piece of your wall pocket. Cut out 1 main piece from the 8½ x 11-inch (22 x 28-cm) piece of felt.

3. Using the cutting templates, create your patterns. Cut 1 flower and 1 leaf piece from the felt pieces.

4. Place the main piece on your work surface. Fold the top edge over 1 inch (2.5 cm). Use a few pins to hold the fold in place. Thread a needle with a length of embroidery thread, and tie a knot at the end. Stitch close to the edge using a running stitch. Tie a knot on the back, and cut the thread. This will create an area for the dowel to slide in. (Photo B)

5. Turn the main fabric piece around so the fold is in the back. Position the pocket piece on top of the main piece. Place a couple of pins to hold in place. Stitch around the sides and bottom using a running stitch. Tie a knot on the back and cut the thread. (Photo C)

6. Center the leaf on the bottom of the pocket piece followed by the flower and button. You do not need to stitch the leaf and flower in place, only the button. Sew the button onto the main piece. (Photo D)

7. Push a dowel through the top channel that you stitched earlier. Tie a long piece of embroidery thread to both ends. (Photo E)

A

B

C

D

E

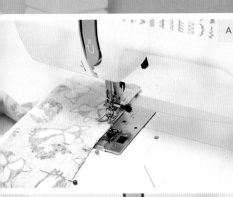

A

B

C

D

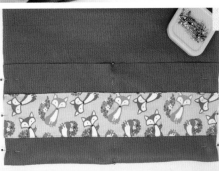

E

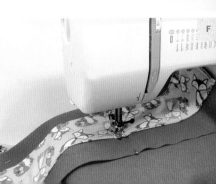

F

BUNK BED BOOK CADDY

A bunk bed book caddy comes in handy when you finish reading your favorite book, but are too sleepy to climb down the ladder to put it away! Just reach over and tuck your book inside one of the pockets. You can use a book caddy on the lower bunk, too!

sewing level: 3

1 (20 x 7-inch [51 x 18-cm]) piece of cotton fabric (optional)

Pins

Sewing machine

Thread

Scissors

Iron

Ironing board

1 (18 x 45-inch [46 x 114-cm]) piece of felt

1. The cotton trim fabric is purely decorative. You can make the caddy without it if you prefer. If using it, fold the cotton fabric in half, with the right sides of the fabric facing each other, so that it measures 20 x 3½ inches (51 x 9 cm). Place pins along the edge every couple of inches to hold it in place.

2. Sew the side seam so that you have a long tube of fabric. Trim any thread that may be hanging off the fabric. (Photo A)

3. Turn the fabric right-side out. Ask an adult to help you iron along the seam so that it is nice and flat.

4. The edges of the fabric band are open and unfinished, so fold the edges over and tuck them inside the tube. Place a pin on each side to close the ends. Set this piece to the side. (Photo B)

5. Fold the 18-inch (46-cm) edge of your felt up 7 inches (18 cm). This will be the pocket for your book caddy. You will unfold it before you sew the decorative fabric on top. For now, you are just making sure everything lines up correctly. Center the cotton fabric band and pin it in place. (Photo C)

6. Unfold the felt. Sew the fabric band to the felt on the top and bottom edges. Leave the ends unstitched, but keep them pinned. Trim any thread that might be hanging off the fabric. (Photo D)

7. Fold the felt up one more time (7 inches [18 cm]) and place pins along the side edges. Sew the side edges using the pressure foot as your guide for your seam allowance. (Photo E)

8. Place 3 pins along the center of the pocket to divide it in half. Stitch from the pin on the bottom and continue to sew until you reach the pin on the top. Trim the threads. (Photo F)

9. Lift the mattress on your bed and slide the book caddy underneath with the pocket hanging over the side.

POM-POM THROW

A warm and cuddly throw perfect for cold mornings, sleepovers and movie nights! Pom-poms are such a fun embellishment. Just make sure to use a lot of pins to hold everything in place while you sew. Soon you'll find yourself adding pom-pom trim to just about everything!

sewing level: 3

1½ yards (1.37 m) of fleece

Scissors

10-inch (25-cm) bowl

Sewing pen

7 yards (6.4 m) of pom-pom trim

Pins

Sewing machine

Walking foot attachment (optional)

Thread

1. Lay the fleece fabric on your work surface. Trim off the printed edges with your scissors. The printed border on the fabric is called a selvage. (Photo A)

2. Fold the fabric in half and then in half again so that it is in quarters. Place a bowl on the edge of the fabric and draw a curve from one side edge to the bottom edge using the sewing pen. (Photo B)

3. Cut along the curve with scissors. This will create rounded corners for the blanket. (Photo C)

4. Unfold the fabric and lay it on your work surface with the right side of the fabric facing you. Line up the pom-pom trim with the edge of the back of the fabric. Place a pin after every 3 pom-poms to keep the trim in place. Continue pinning until you have reached the beginning point again. (Photo D)

5. Slightly overlap the pom-pom trim where the end meets the beginning, and pin it in place.

If your sewing machine has a walking foot attachment, you can use it to stitch the pom-pom trim to the fleece. A walking foot helps feed the fabric evenly through the sewing machine when you are sewing layers of thick fabric. If you do not have one, that is okay, just stitch slowly and check often to make sure that your fabric isn't bunching or puckering as you go.

6. Line up the pressure foot on your sewing machine with the edge of the fabric. Stitch around the entire throw. Go slowly, removing the pins as your needle gets near them, and make sure that the pom-pom trim is always even with the edge of the back of the fabric. (Photo E)

7. When you reach the beginning again, sew in reverse for a few stitches and cut the threads. (Photo F)

Have a great day !!
♥ Mom

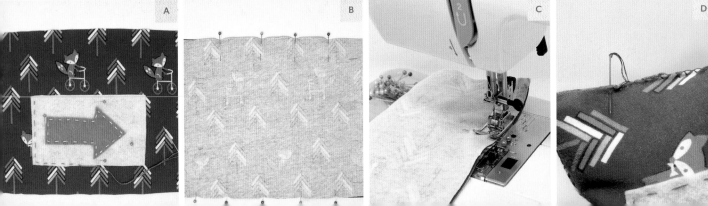

MESSAGE PILLOW

A message pillow is a great place to receive special notes from members of your family. It works even better if everyone has one on their bed! The pocket is just the right size to leave a card or note telling them to have a great day or how much you care about them. Be sure to check yours to see if anyone left you a note, too!

sewing level: 2

Arrow template (page 175)

Scissors

1 (8 x 5-inch [20 x 13-cm]) piece of felt for the arrow

Pins

1 (6 x 4-inch [15 x 10-cm]) rectangle of felt for the pocket

Embroidery thread

Needle

2 (8½ x 11-inch [22 x 28-cm]) pieces of cotton fabric for the pillow (see note)

Sewing machine

Thread

Stuffing

NOTE
You can use a sheet of copy paper as a cutting template for pillow pieces.

1. Using the cutting template, create your pattern. Cut out 1 arrow from the felt.

2. Pin the arrow to the center of the felt pocket. Cut a length of embroidery thread, and tie a knot at one end. Thread the other end through a needle. Stitch along the edge of the fabric using a running stitch. Tie a knot and cut the thread.

3. Pin the rectangle to the center of 1 of the pillow pieces. Stitch along the sides and bottom. Tie a knot and cut the thread. (Photo A)

4. Place the pillow piece with the pocket on your work surface. Make sure the printed side of the fabric is facing you. Place the other pillow piece on top. The wrong side of the fabric should be facing you. This might not look right to you, but don't worry, it is!

5. To keep everything together while you sew, place pins every few inches all the way around. Make sure to leave a section open so that you can turn your pillow right-side out after you sew! (Photo B)

   It sometimes helps to place 2 pins on each side of the opening for your stuffing. This will help you remember to stop sewing when you get to the double pins.

6. Use the sewing machine pressure foot as a guide, keeping your fabric lined up with it as you sew. When you get to a corner, make sure that the needle is down in the fabric before you lift the pressure foot to turn the fabric. After you turn the fabric, lower the pressure foot again and continue sewing. Start machine sewing at one set of double pins and continue around the entire pillow until you reach the second set of double pins. Trim the threads. (Photo C)

7. After sewing all the sides, carefully trim a small triangle off each corner. Make sure not to cut too closely to the seam. Trimming corners creates a finished look when the pillow is turned right-side out.

8. Turn the pillow right-side out.

9. Grab a few handfuls of stuffing and put it inside the pillow using the opening on the side. Continue stuffing the pillow until it is as firm as you'd like.

10. Fold the sides of the opening over to hide unfinished fabric edges. Pin in place.

11. Cut a long length of thread. Thread a needle, bring both ends together and tie a knot. Stitch the opening closed with a whipstitch. Tie a knot and cut the thread. (Photo D)

SEW-PHISTICATED GIFTS TO MAKE

×××××××◯

"It's not how much we give but how much love we put into giving."

—Mother Teresa

This chapter is full of simple gifts to make for your family and friends. Whether it's a Hand-Stitched Card (page 71) or a Burp Cloth (page 72) for a new baby, the thoughtfulness behind your gift will be cherished forever!

A

B

C

D

Reach for the Stars

you are
DINO-Mite!

HAND-STITCHED CARDS

Did you know that you can sew paper? It's fun and easy to create your own greeting cards with hand-stitched details for any occasion!

sewing level: 1

3 (8½ x 11-inch [22 x 28-cm]) pieces of cardstock paper

Scissors

Cookie cutter

Pencil

Potholder

Pushpin

Needle

Embroidery thread

Double-sided tape or a glue stick

1. Fold a piece of cardstock in half. Cut along the fold with scissors. Now you can make 2 cards.

2. Lightly trace around a cookie cutter in the center of each piece of cardstock. Make sure to use a pencil so that you can erase the pencil markings later. (Photo A)

3. Place your paper on top of a potholder to protect your surface while you poke sewing holes into it. Use your pushpin to poke evenly spaced holes around the edge of your drawing. (Photo B)

4. Erase any pencil markings.

5. Thread your needle with a long length of embroidery thread. Use all 6 strands so that your stitches stand out. Because your thread is so thick, you may want to ask an adult to help you thread your needle. Tie a knot at one end.

6. Poke your needle through the back into one of the holes and begin stitching all the way around. When you have finished stitching, tie a knot in your thread close to the paper and trim off any extra thread. (Photo C)

7. Add any decorative details you'd like! Maybe a speech bubble, some grass or a sun. The possibilities are endless! (Photo D)

8. Fold the other two pieces of cardstock in half. Use double-sided tape to attach your hand-stitched drawings to the other pieces of cardstock to create 2 cards.

BURP CLOTH

Here is a gift to make for a baby brother or sister! Made out of flannel, these burp cloths are soft and absorbent, and very simple to make.

sewing level: 3

Burp cloth template (page 161)

¼ yard (0.23 m) flannel for the front

¼ yard (0.23 m) flannel for the back

Pins

Scissors

Sewing machine

Thread

1. Fold 1 piece of flannel in half. Place the cutting template on the fold, pin in place and cut around the template. Repeat for the other piece of flannel.

2. Unfold both pieces of fabric. Place one on top of the other with the right sides of the fabric facing out. Pin the front and back together around the edges of the fabric. (Photo A)

3. Sew all along the edge using the pressure foot on your sewing machine as a guide.

4. Make ½-inch (13-mm)-wide cuts all along the edge. Be careful to cut close to your seam, but not on the seam. (Photo B)

5. Machine wash the burp cloth and tumble dry. When it comes out of the dryer, the edges will be fringed and fluffy, which is what you want. Trim off any long, loose strings.

6. Each time the burp cloth is washed and dried, the edges become more fringed and fluffy!

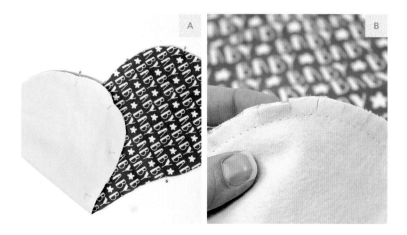

PUPPY PLACE MAT

We all know that puppies can drool and be a bit messy when it comes to mealtime. Make a cute place mat to catch the drips! It even has places to put the water and food bowl.

sewing level: 3

4 (8-inch [20-cm]) circles of cotton fabric

Measuring tape

Scissors

Pins

Sewing machine

Thread

Iron

Ironing board

1 (14 x 20-inch [36 x 51-cm]) piece of cotton for the front of the place mat

1 (14 x 20-inch [36 x 51-cm]) piece of low-loft quilt batting

1 (14 x 20-inch [36 x 51-cm]) piece of cotton for the back of the place mat

1. Fold 1 circle in half. Cut a 2-inch (5-cm) slit in the center of the fold. Place this circle on top of another circle with the right sides of the fabric facing each other. Add a few pins to keep the 2 circles together. Sew around the entire edge using the pressure foot on your sewing machine as a guide. (Photo A)

2. Use your scissors to cut small slits every ½ inch (13 mm) around the circle edge. Be careful not to cut the stitching. This will help create a finished edge when you turn your circle right-side out. (Photo B)

3. Turn the circle right-side out through the opening that you made when you made the 2-inch (5-cm) cut in the fold. Ask an adult to help you iron around the edges.

4. Repeat with the other 2 circles. You should now have 2 appliques to sew onto the front of the place mat.

5. Pin each circle applique to the front of the place mat. Sew close to the edge (⅛ inch [3 mm]) around each circle. Trim the threads. (Photo C)

6. Place the piece of batting on your work surface. Lay the front of the place mat on top with the circles facing you. Place the coordinating rectangle of fabric on top, with the right side of the fabric facing down. You should have 3 rectangles stacked together at this point. Place pins around the edges to keep everything in place. (Photo D)

7. Leave a small opening for turning your place mat right-side out. It sometimes helps to place 2 pins on each side of the opening. This will help you remember to stop sewing when you get to the double pins. (Photo E)

8. Start sewing at one set of double pins and continue around your entire place mat until you reach the second set of double pins. Use your sewing machine pressure foot as a guide, keeping your fabric lined up with it as you sew. When you get to a corner, make sure that the needle is down in the fabric before you lift the pressure foot to turn the fabric. After you turn the fabric, lower the pressure foot again and continue sewing. Trim the threads.

9. After sewing all sides, carefully trim a small triangle off each corner. Make sure not to cut too closely to your seam. This step will create a finished edge when you turn the place mat right-side out.

10. Turn your place mat right-side out through the opening. Ask an adult to help you iron the edges of the place mat. Fold the edges of the opening down and pin together.

11. Topstitch a ⅛-inch (3-mm) seam around the entire edge of the place mat. Trim the threads.

APPLE GIFT-CARD HOLDER

This apple is just the right size to hold a gift card for your teacher! A fun little way to say "thank you" at the end of the school year or on Teacher Appreciation Day!

sewing level: 1

Apple templates (page 157)

Scissors

1 (10 x 5-inch [25 x 13-cm]) rectangle of red felt for the apple

3 x 3-inch (8 x 8-cm) squares of green, brown and black felt for the stem, leaf and heart

Measuring tape

White and red embroidery thread

Needle

Pins

1. Using the cutting templates, create your patterns. Cut out 2 apple shapes, 1 stem, 1 leaf and 1 heart.

2. Fold 1 of the apple shapes in half, horizontally, and cut a 1¾-inch (4-cm) slit on the fold. When you unfold your apple, you will have a 3½-inch (9-cm) slit in the center. Set this piece to the side. (Photo A)

3. Cut a length of white embroidery thread and thread the needle with one end. Tie a knot at the other end. Use a running stitch to sew the heart to the other apple shape so that it resembles a tiny chalkboard. (Photo B)

4. Place the apple shape with a slit on your work surface. Overlap the leaf and stem piece on the top edge of the apple by ½ inch (13 mm) and place the other apple shape on top. Add a few pins to keep everything together. (Photo C)

5. Cut a length of red embroidery thread and thread the needle with one end. Tie a knot at the other end. Stitch around the apple using a running stitch. Tie a knot on the back, and cut the thread.

A

B

C

FISHING TOY FOR CATS

Make your kitty a fun toy to play with! Dangle the fishing pole, and watch him jump to try and catch the fish!

sewing level: 1

Fish templates (page 163)

Scissors

1 (8 x 4-inch [20 x 10-cm]) rectangle of felt for the fish

1 (3 x 1-inch [8 x 2.5-cm]) rectangle for felt strip

Embroidery thread

Needle

Pin

Dowel

1. Using the cutting templates, create your patterns. Cut out 2 fish shapes.

2. Fold the rectangle strip of felt in half. Pin in between the 2 fish shapes where the mouth of the fish would be. (Photo A)

3. Cut a length of embroidery thread, and tie a knot at one end. Thread a needle with the other end. Stitch around the entire fish using a running stitch. Tie a knot and cut the thread.

4. Cut a long piece of embroidery thread. String one end of the thread through the loop on the fish and tie a knot. (Photo B)

5. Tie the other end to the dowel with a double knot. (Photo C)

6. For fun, try stitching on an eye or fins!

GIFT BAG

This little gift bag is so easy to customize! Make a couple of them in this size. Then experiment with larger and smaller squares of felt to create different sizes. You can make them to fit all sorts of goodies for friends and family members!

sewing level: 1

Star template (page 181)

Scissors

1 (5 x 5-inch [13 x 13-cm]) square of felt for the star

Pins

2 (5½ x 6-inch [14 x 15-cm]) pieces of felt for the bag

Embroidery thread

Needle

2 (1 x 10-inch [2.5 x 25-cm) pieces of felt for the handles

1. Using the cutting template, create your pattern. Cut out a star.

2. Pin the star onto 1 of the main bag pieces. Thread a needle with a length of embroidery thread. Tie a knot at one end. Sew around the star using a running stitch. Tie a knot and cut the thread. (Photo A)

3. Pin 1 handle piece to the front, placing it 1 inch (2.5 cm) from each edge. (Photo A)

4. Repeat with the other main bag piece and handle. (Photo A)

5. Cut a long length of embroidery thread. Tie a knot at one end, and thread the other end through a needle. Using 2 long stitches, sew an X across the middle of each end of the handle. Tie a knot, cut the thread and tie a new knot in the thread as you move on to each X. Leave the pins in as you stitch the X so that your handles don't accidentally move out of place. (Photo B)

6. Pin the main pieces together to keep everything in place. (Photo C)

7. Stitch around the sides and bottom of the bag using a whipstitch. Trim the thread.

CUTE AS A BUTTON ACCESSORIES

Whether you are dressing for the weather or wanting to look like a rock star, having the right accessories is a MUST, and this chapter is chock-full of them! Own the first day of school with a Gathered Flower Headband (page 85) that matches your outfit. Carry your summer essentials to the beach in a Watermelon Tote (page 97), or stay warm on chilly days with a fleece Ear Warmer (page 104).

GATHERED FLOWER HEADBAND

These gathered flowers are a great project for using up fabric scraps. They take just minutes to make and are fun to customize! Add one to an elastic headband for a one-of-a-kind hair accessory!

sewing level: 1

Needle

Embroidery thread

1 (7-inch [18-cm]) circle of cotton fabric

1 (4-inch [10-cm]) circle of cotton fabric

Scissors

1-inch (2.5-cm) button

Hot glue gun

2-inch (5-cm) circle of felt

Elastic headband

1. Thread a needle with embroidery thread, and tie a knot at the other end. Using a running stitch, sew around the edge of each circle. Do not cut the thread. (Photo A)

2. Pull the 2 end strings tight, and your circle will gather up. (Photo B)

3. Tie the strings into a double knot and trim the thread. (Photo C)

4. Stack the 2 layers together with the gathered side facing up.

5. Thread a needle, bring both ends together and tie a knot at the end. Sew a button in the center of the 2 layers. Tie a knot on the back and trim the thread. (Photo D)

6. Ask an adult to help you add a drop of hot glue onto the center of the felt circle. Place the elastic headband on top of the glue drop. Add a few more drizzles of glue and press the flower firmly on top. (Photo E)

NOTE

You can create these beautiful flowers in any size you'd like! The finished flower size will always be half the size of the circle that you cut out. For example: the 7-inch (18-cm) and 4-inch (10-cm) circles used in this project created a flower with 3½-inch (9-cm) and 2-inch (5-cm) layers. You can use cereal bowls, jars, cups and other round objects as patterns for your circles. There are so many uses for these pretty flowers. Glue a magnet or pin to the back, or sew a few onto a pillow or t-shirt!

ANIMAL SLEEP MASK

Sleep masks are great for blocking out light and helping you fall asleep at night! We'll make a pig together, but you can make five different animal friends using this simple template. Mix up the colors, add your own details and have fun!

sewing level: 2

makes 1 mask, with 5 animal template options

Sleep Mask templates (page 155 and 157)

Scissors

1 (8 x 8-inch [20 x 20-cm]) rectangle of felt for the sleep mask

A variety of felt scraps for the facial details (2–6-inch [5–15-cm] squares and rectangles)

Needle

Embroidery thread

Pencil or sewing pen

Pins

1 (11-inch [28-cm]) piece of ⅛-inch (3-mm) elastic

Sewing machine

Thread

1. Using the cutting templates, create your patterns. Cut out 2 sleep mask pieces, 2 outer ears, 2 inner ears and 1 nose for the pig.

2. Stack 1 outer and 1 inner ear piece together. Thread a needle with a long length of embroidery thread, and tie a knot at the other end. You can use this same color of embroidery thread for the entire project. Use a running stitch to sew around the edges with embroidery thread, leaving the bottom open. Tie a knot and trim the thread. Repeat with the other 2 ear pieces. Set aside. (Photo A)

3. Mark a 1-inch (2.5-cm) curve for each eye on 1 of the sleep mask pieces using a pencil or sewing pen. Stitch along the curve using a backstitch. Add a few eyelash stitches under the curve. Repeat for the other eye. Do not tie a knot or cut the thread just yet. (Photo B)

4. Stitch the nose onto the center of the sleep mask piece. Add 2 stitches for the nostrils. Tie a knot on the back and trim off any extra thread.

5. Lay the bottom sleep mask piece on your work surface. Place the ears on top. Lay the top sleep mask piece over the ears. Pin the ears in place. (Photo C)

6. Slide the ends of the elastic in between the top and bottom sleep mask pieces. Pin into place. (Photo D)

7. Sew a ⅛-inch (3-mm) seam allowance all the way around the sleep mask. Go slowly around the rounded areas. When you get to the area under the nose, you will want to change the direction of the fabric. Make sure that your needle is in the fabric, and lift the pressure foot on your sewing machine to turn the fabric. Lower the pressure foot back down and continue sewing. Trim the thread.

NOTE

Here are the cutting instructions for the other animal masks.

Owl: Cut 4 ears, 1 head piece, 2 eyes and 1 beak

Dog: Cut 2 ears, 1 nose and 1 mouth

Polar Bear: Cut 2 outer ears, 2 inner ears and 1 nose

Mouse: Cut 2 outer ears, 2 inner ears and 1 nose

Get creative with the details! You can even use buttons or other accessories to create the animal faces. Can you think of any other animals to make using this template?

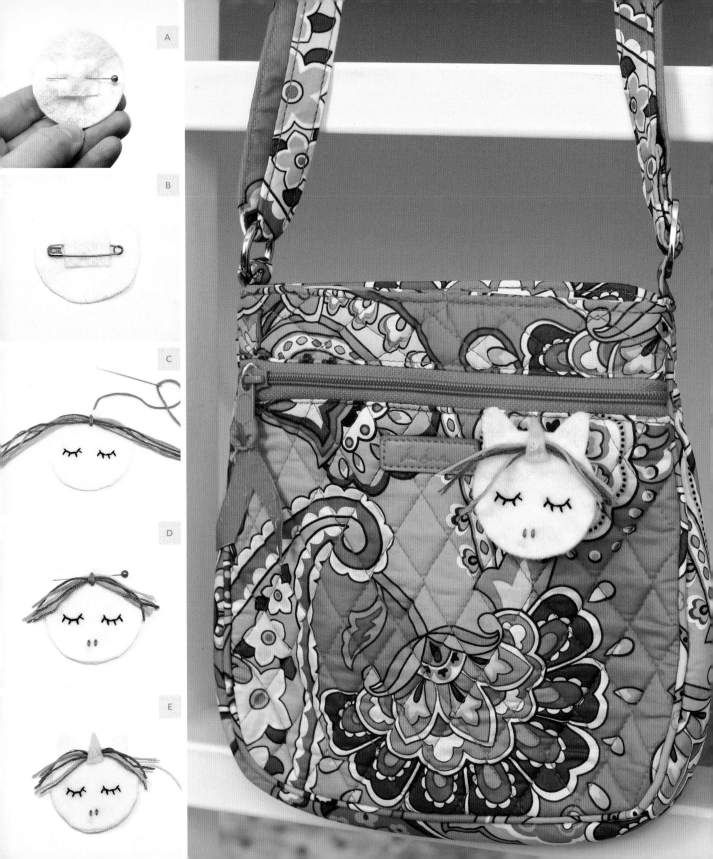

A

B

C

D

E

UNICORN PIN

This magical little unicorn is just the right size to pin to your jacket or backpack. Get creative with the embroidery thread to create a custom mane using your favorite colors!

sewing level: 1

Unicorn templates (page 183)

Scissors

1 (6 x 3-inch [15 x 8-cm]) rectangle of felt for the unicorn head

2-inch (5-cm) scraps of felt for the ears, horn and safety pin slide

Pins

Embroidery thread

Needle

Safety pin

1. Using the cutting templates, create your patterns. Cut out 2 circles for the unicorn head, 2 ears, 1 horn and 1 small rectangle.

2. Pin the small rectangle to the center of one of the circles. (Photo A)

3. Thread the needle with a length of embroidery thread, and tie a knot at the end. Use a running stitch to sew across the top of the rectangle. Tie a knot on the back and cut the thread. Then sew across the bottom of the rectangle. Tie a knot at the back, and cut the thread. (Photo B)

4. Slip an open safety pin through one side. Close the safety pin and set the circle to the side. (Photo B)

5. Place the other circle onto your work surface. Thread the needle with a length of embroidery thread, and tie a knot at the end. Using a backstitch, stitch 4 stitches in a semicircle shape for each eye. Add 4 more stitches for the eyelashes. Tie a knot on the back, and cut the thread. (Photo C)

6. Cut 5 to 6 short strands of embroidery thread in a variety of colors. Lay them across the top of the circle for the mane. Cut a length of embroidery thread, thread the needle and tie a knot at the end. Sew a couple of stitches on top of each other in the center of the mane to hold the thread in place. Tie a knot at the back, and cut the thread. Give the mane a little haircut, and trim the thread to any length you'd like. (Photo C)

7. Cut another length of thread, thread your needle and tie a knot at the end. Stitch 2 small stitches toward the bottom for the nostrils. Tie a knot at the back, and cut the thread. (Photo D)

8. Place the other felt circle on your work surface with the safety pin on the back. Place the second felt circle with the unicorn face on top. Tuck the ears in between the 2 circles and add a pin to hold them in place. Cut a long length of embroidery thread, thread the needle and tie a knot at the end. Use a running stitch to stitch around the face. Tie a knot on the back, and cut the thread. (Photo D)

9. Place the horn in the center of the mane, and stitch an X through the center of the horn. Add a few stitches all around to keep everything secure. (Photo E)

HAIR SCRUNCHIE

Here is a great way to use up some of those fabric scraps that you've collected from all of your sewing projects. Hair scrunchies are easy to make, and they are fun to give as gifts! Use them to hold a ponytail, or wrap one on your wrist like a bracelet!

sewing level: 3

1 (4 x 20-inch [10 x 51-cm]) rectangle of fabric

Measuring tape

Pins

Sewing machine

Thread

Scissors

2 safety pins

1 (9-inch [23-cm]) piece of ¼-inch (6-mm)-wide elastic

1. Fold the rectangle of fabric in half lengthwise with the right sides of the fabric facing each other. Use the measuring tape to measure 3 inches (8 cm) from the top. Mark that spot with a pin and repeat for the bottom. (Photo A)

2. Sew the side seam starting at the top pin and continuing until you reach the bottom pin. Use the pressure foot on your sewing machine as a guide. Do not sew above the top pin or below the bottom pin.

3. Turn the scrunchie right-side out. This can sometimes be a little difficult when you are working with such a small opening. You may want to ask an adult to help with this part. (Photo B)

4. Now it's time to turn the long tube of fabric into a circle! Bring the ends together with the right sides of the fabric touching, and add a couple of pins to keep everything together. (Photo B)

5. Sew across the top using the pressure foot on the sewing machine as a guide.

6. You should now have a round tube of fabric with a 5-inch (13-cm) opening along the side. Use a safety pin to pin one end of the elastic near the opening. Attach the other safety pin to the other end of the elastic. Use the safety pin as a guide to push the elastic into the opening and all the way around until it comes out the other side. (Photo C)

7. Remove both safety pins, and tie the ends of the elastic into a double knot. (Photo D)

8. Fold the edges of the side opening over ¼ inch (6 mm) on both sides. Add a few pins to keep the edges together. Sew close to the edge of the fabric (about a ⅛-inch [3-mm] seam allowance). Trim the threads. (Photo E)

A

B

C

D

E

LITTLE BAKER'S APRON

Make an apron with a pocket to keep a recipe card or measuring spoons in while you bake!

sewing level: 3

2 (16 x 14-inch [41 x 36-cm]) rectangles of fabric for the apron

1 (5-inch [13-cm]) cereal bowl

Sewing pen

Scissors

2 (11 x 6-inch [28 x 15-cm]) rectangles of cotton fabric for the pocket

Pins

Sewing machine

Thread

Iron

Ironing board

1 (64-inch [163-cm]) piece of ⅞-inch (22-mm)-wide ribbon

1. Fold each of the 16 x 14-inch (41 x 36-cm) rectangles in half width-wise. Use a small bowl to trace a curve along the side and bottom edge with a sewing pen. Cut along the curve. Open the fabric along the fold and set aside. Repeat for the 11 x 6-inch (28 x 15-cm) rectangles. (Photo A)

2. Pin the 16 x 14-inch (41 x 36-cm) rectangles together with the right sides of the fabric facing each other. Leave an opening along the bottom to turn the apron right-side out when you have finished sewing along the edges. It sometimes helps to place 2 pins on each side of the opening. This will help you remember to stop sewing when you get to the double pins. Repeat with the 11 x 6-inch (28 x 15-cm) rectangles for the pocket. (Photo B)

3. Start sewing at one set of double pins, and sew all the way around the apron piece using the pressure foot on your sewing machine as a guide. Repeat with the pocket piece. Trim the threads.

4. Carefully trim a small triangle off each corner. Make sure not to cut too closely to your seam. Use your scissors to cut small slits every ½ inch (13 mm) around the rounded edge. Be careful to not cut the stitching. This will help keep the edges round when you turn the circle right-side out. Do this for both the apron piece and the pocket piece.

5. Turn both pieces right-side out. Ask an adult to help you press the seams with an iron.

6. Fold the edges of the opening over and pin to close. Repeat for the pocket piece.

7. Center the pocket piece onto the front of the apron piece. Add a few pins to keep it in place. Sew the pocket to the apron by topstitching close to the edge (⅛- to ¼-inch [3- to 6-mm] seam allowance). Do not sew across the top of the pocket. Trim the threads. (Photo C)

8. Topstitch a ¼-inch (6-mm) seam around the sides and bottom of the apron piece. Trim the threads.

9. Fold the 64-inch (163-cm) piece of ribbon in half. Place the fold on the center of the top apron edge. Open the ribbon and add a pin to keep it centered. Add a few additional pins along the top. Sew the ribbon to the apron along the top AND bottom edges using a ¼-inch (6-mm) seam allowance. Trim the threads. (Photo D)

10. Ask an adult to lightly burn the ends of the ribbon using a lighter. This will melt the ends enough to keep them from fraying in the future.

SUNGLASSES CASE

Sunglasses can easily get scratched and dirty if they are left in a backpack or beach tote. Make a case out of colorful felt and a piece of ribbon to protect them!

sewing level: 3

1 (8-inch [20-cm]) square of felt

2 (8-inch [20-cm]) pieces of ½-inch (13-mm)-wide ribbon

Pins

Sewing machine

Thread

Scissors

1. Place the square of felt on your work surface.

2. Lay 1 piece of ribbon 1 inch from the top. Add a couple of pins to keep it in place. Lay the second piece just below and pin in place. (Photo A)

3. Using the sewing machine, stitch through the center of each piece of ribbon. (Photo B)

4. Fold the 8-inch (20-cm) square in half with the ribbon on the outside. Place a few pins along the side and bottom edge. (Photo C)

5. Sew the side and bottom edge, using your sewing machine pressure foot as a guide.

6. Cut the thread. Trim close to the stitching with scissors for a nice, clean edge.

WATERMELON TOTE

This handy little tote is the perfect size for so many things. Use it for books, shopping, a day at the beach and more! If you are new to using a sewing machine, this is a great beginning project to make with an adult. No curves, just straight line sewing!

sewing level: 2
makes a 12 x 13½-inch
(30 x 34-cm) tote

2 (13 x 10-inch [33 x 25-cm]) rectangles of pink fabric

2 (13 x 2-inch [33 x 5-cm]) rectangles of white fabric

Pins

2 (13 x 4-inch [33 x 10-cm]) rectangles of green fabric

Sewing machine

Thread

Scissors

Iron

Ironing board

Measuring tape

1 (4 x 6-inch [10 x 15-cm]) rectangle of black felt for the watermelon seeds

Needle

Embroidery thread

2 (20-inch [51-cm]) pieces of 1-inch (2.5-cm)-wide pink cotton belting

1. Lay 1 of the pink rectangles on your work surface with the right side of the fabric facing you. Place 1 of the white rectangles on top of the pink fabric, with the right sides of the fabric touching each other and lining up the bottom edges. Add a few pins to keep the 2 pieces together. (Photo A)

2. With the right sides together, add the green rectangle to the bottom of the white rectangle and pin to keep everything together. Sew these 2 pieces together using the sewing machine pressure foot as a guide. (Photo A)

3. Sew the pink and white pieces together using the sewing machine pressure foot as a guide. Trim the threads.

4. Ask an adult to help you iron the seams flat. (Photo B)

5. You should now have what resembles a square slice of watermelon! Green on the bottom, a small strip of white and pink on the top. Repeat this process with the other 3 rectangles until you have 2 square slices of watermelon.

6. Fold the pink top edge over ½ inch (13 mm). Ask an adult to help you iron it nice and flat. Fold one more time so that you have a nice, smooth double fold. Add a few pins to hold the fold in place. Sew across the top, stitching close to the bottom edge. Repeat for the other watermelon piece. Trim the threads. (Photo C)

7. Cut out 3 watermelon seed shapes from the black scrap of felt (1½ to 2 inches [4 to 5 cm]). Decide which of the rectangle watermelon slices you want for the front of your bag. Pin the seeds into place. Thread a needle with a length of embroidery thread, and tie a knot at the end. Hand stitch the seeds to the front of your bag using a running stitch. Tie a knot on the back, and cut the thread. (Photo D)

8. With the right sides of the fabric facing each other, pin the front of the bag to the back along the edges. Machine stitch along the sides and the bottom using the pressure foot on your sewing machine as a guide. Using scissors, trim closely to the stitching to tidy up the edge.

9. Trim the bottom corners on a diagonal, but do not cut your stitching. This will make the corners nice and finished when you turn the bag right-side out.

10. Zigzag stitch around the edge to catch any loose threads and to prevent the edge from fraying in the future, if desired.

(continued)

11. Turn the bag right-side out.

12. The 2 (20-inch [51 cm]) pieces of cotton belting are for the tote handles. One is for the front handle, and one is for the back.

    Place each end on the inside of the tote 2 inches (5 cm) from the side and 2 inches (5 cm) from the top. Place 2 pins, one just under the top hem of the bag and the other just above the edge of the handle piece. (Photo E)

13. Sew from the top pin to the bottom, keeping your stitches close to the edge of the handle. Raise the pressure foot with the needle still in your fabric and adjust your fabric so that it is facing you once more. Continue to sew and adjust at each corner until you have stitched a square. This will create a strong hold for each end of the handle. Repeat for the other tote handle. (Photo F)

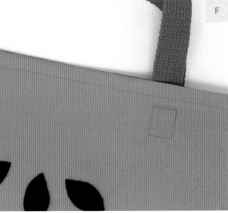

CROSSBODY BAG

An everyday bag to carry your essentials! The strap is long enough to cross over your body, making it sturdy and easy to carry around.

sewing level: 3

1 (4 x 42-inch [10 x 107-cm]) rectangle of fabric for the strap

Pins

Sewing machine

Thread

Iron

Ironing board

1 (8-inch [20-cm]) piece of ⅞-inch (22-mm)-wide Velcro

2 (10 x 12-inch [25 x 31-cm]) rectangles of fabric for the lining

2 (10 x 12-inch [25 x 31-cm]) rectangles of fabric for the outer bag

Scissors

Measuring tape

1. This step can sometimes be a little difficult when you are working with such a small opening. You may want to ask an adult to help with this part.

   Fold the strap piece in half with the right-side of the fabric on the inside. Place pins along the side edge. Sew the side seam using the pressure foot on your sewing machine as a guide. Turn the strap right-side out. (Photo A)

2. Ask an adult to help you iron the strap flat, with the seam on the side. Topstitch both sides of the strap close to the edge using a ⅛-inch (3-mm) seam allowance. (Photo B)

3. Separate your piece of Velcro into two sections: a scratchy one and a soft one. Place one section of Velcro 1 inch (2.5 cm) from the top edge on each of the lining pieces of fabric. Pin in place. Sew close to the edge of the Velcro. When you get to a corner, keep the needle in the fabric and raise the pressure foot. Pivot the fabric, lower the pressure foot and continue to sew. Do this for each corner of the Velcro until you reach the starting point. This will form a rectangle of stitches. Trim the threads. (Photo C)

4. Pin the outer pieces of fabric together with the right-side of the fabric on the inside. Sew around the side and bottom edges using the pressure foot on your sewing machine as a guide. When you get to a corner, keep the needle in the fabric and raise the pressure foot. Pivot the fabric, lower the pressure foot and continue to sew. Trim the bottom corners on a diagonal, but do not trim your stitching. This will make the corners nice and finished when you turn the bag right-side out. Repeat with the lining pieces of fabric.

5. Turn the outer bag right-side out. Do not turn the lining right-side out. Fold the top edge of both bag sections ½ inch (13 mm) down and press with an iron. (Photo D)

(continued)

crossbody bag (continued)

6. Slide the lining of the bag inside the outer bag, with the top edge of the lining just under the top edge of the outer bag. Pin the side seams together, then add pins all along the top edge. (Photo E)

7. Your strap is 42 inches (107 cm) long, but you might want it to be a little shorter depending on how tall you are. Remove the side seam pins and slide one end of the strap in between the lining and outer layer, about 1 inch (2.5 cm). Pin the ends of the strap into place.

8. Try wearing the bag across your shoulders and body. If you like the length of the strap, great! If you want to shorten it, remove 1 of the side pins and adjust the strap to a length that is comfortable for you. Then trim the strap and pin it back into place.

9. Sew around the top of the bag using a ¼-inch (6-mm) seam allowance or close to the top edge of the lining. Trim the threads. (Photo F)

UNICORN MANE SCARF

A warm and cozy scarf to wear on a chilly day. Wrap it around your neck, and you'll instantly be magical and colorful like a unicorn!

sewing level: 3

¼ yard (0.23 m) pink fleece

¼ yard (0.23 m) turquoise fleece

¼ yard (0.23 m) purple fleece

Measuring tape

Scissors

Pins

Sewing machine

Thread

Small piece of paper

1. Cut a strip of fleece that is 5 inches (13 cm) wide and 48 inches (122 cm) long from each color. (Photo A)

2. Layer the 3 fleece strips flat on top of each other. Place pins along the center of the fleece starting at the top and continuing to the bottom. (Photo B)

3. Use your sewing machine to sew a straight line through the middle. It's okay if the line isn't perfectly straight. This project is very forgiving! Just do your best. Trim the threads. (Photo C)

4. Cut 1-inch (2.5-cm)-wide slits along both sides of the scarf. Make sure not to cut the stitching in the middle! You can make a cutting template from a 1-inch (2.5-cm)-wide and 2½-inch (6-cm)-long piece of scratch paper. This will create even slits as you cut. (Photo D)

5. Pick up your scarf and give it a really good shake. It will fluff up, and you will be able to see all 3 colors!

EAR WARMER

Keep your ears warm and cozy with a stretchy fleece ear warmer! If you had fun making the Hair Scrunchies (page 90) you'll LOVE this project! The process is almost the same.

sewing level: 3

1 (8 x 20-inch [20 x 51-cm]) rectangle of fleece (see note)

Measuring tape

Pins

Sewing machine

Thread

Scissors

1. Fold the rectangle of fabric in half, so that it creates a 20-inch (51-cm) tube of fabric, with the right sides of the fabric facing each other. Use the measuring tape to measure 3 inches (8 cm) from the top. Mark that spot with a pin and repeat for the bottom. (Photo A)

2. Use the zigzag stitch on your sewing machine for the entire project.

   Sew the side seam starting at the top pin and continuing until you reach the bottom pin. Use the pressure foot on your sewing machine as a guide. Do not sew above the top pin or below the bottom pin.

3. Turn the rectangle right-side out.

4. Now it's time to turn the long tube of fabric into a circle! Bring the ends together with the right sides of the fabric touching, and add a couple of pins to keep everything together. Sew across the top, using the pressure foot on the sewing machine as a guide. (Photo B)

5. You should now have a round tube of fabric with an opening along the side.

6. Fold the edges of the side opening over about ¼ inch (6 mm) on both sides. Add a few pins to keep the edges together. (Photo C)

7. If you have the option to remove the platform on your sewing machine, go ahead and take it off. This will create extra room when sewing around small areas such as sleeves, pant legs or this project.

8. Topstitch close to the edge of the fabric (about ⅛-inch [3-mm] seam allowance) around the entire edge. Repeat on the other side. Trim the threads. (Photo D)

NOTE

This ear warmer will fit ages 6 to 12. For 12+, increase the measurement to 8 x 21 inches (20 x 53 cm) for the rectangle of fleece.

Fleece fabric is stretchy. Give it a little tug and see for yourself! When cutting out your rectangle, make sure that the stretch is going from top to bottom, and not side to side. If you aren't sure if your fleece is facing the right direction, ask an adult to double-check it with you!

HOLIDAY CRAFTS IN A SNAP

xxxxxx〜〜

Birthday celebrations, Christmas and Halloween. What's your favorite day of the year? You'll find seasonal projects that cover these—and every holiday in between—in this chapter! Sew your own not-so-spooky Frankenstein Door Hanger (page 118) for Halloween. Create a Christmas Tree Advent Calendar (page 125) to count down the days until Christmas and make a Rainbow Pom-Pom Garland (page 133) to hang up for a birthday.

TEAR-APART VALENTINE CANDY POUCHES

These candy pouches make great little gifts for friends! Write a note on the front and fill it with candy. When you want to open one, just tear it in half!

sewing level: 1

Heart template (page 183)

Scissors

Pencil

Brown paper lunch bag (6 x 10½-inch [15 x 27-cm] standard size)

Markers or crayons (optional)

Pot holder

Pushpin

Paper clip (optional)

Needle

Embroidery thread

Candy

1. Using the cutting template, create your pattern. Trace 2 hearts onto a brown paper lunch bag with the pencil. Cut out the 2 hearts and set 1 to the side.

2. Decorate the front of the other heart using markers or crayons, if desired.

3. Match up both hearts and place them on top of a pot holder. Use a pushpin to punch evenly spaced holes all the way around the edge of the heart. (Photo A)

4. A paper clip can be useful for holding the 2 hearts together while you sew, but it is optional.

   Thread a needle with embroidery thread, tie a knot at the end and push the needle through the back of one of the holes. Stitch around the heart. (Photo B)

5. When you get toward the end, add a small handful of candy and continue to stitch until you reach the beginning again. Tie a knot and cut off any extra thread.

   To open the candy pouch, just tear it in half!

SWEET-HEART TREAT BAGS

Roses are red, violets are blue
I spy cute Valentine's bags. Do you?
These little treat bags take just minutes to make and are just the right size to fill with treats to pass out on Valentine's Day! You can also use them as party favor bags at a birthday party or fill them with goodies to give to your teacher during the holidays!

sewing level: 2

Heart templates (page 167)

Pinking shears

Scissors

Felt scraps for the hearts

2 (5 x 10-inch [13 x 25-cm]) rectangles of fabric

Pins

Needle

Embroidery thread

Sewing machine

Thread

1 (14-inch [36-cm]) piece of ½-inch (13-mm)-wide ribbon

1. Using the cutting templates, create your patterns. Cut out 1 larger heart from felt using pinking shears and 1 smaller heart using scissors.

   If you do not have pinking shears, you can use scissors. Pinking shears add a decorative edge and when used to cut cotton fabric, they prevent the edge from fraying.

2. Place the larger heart 1½ inches (4 cm) from the bottom of 1 of the rectangles of fabric. Place the smaller heart on top of the larger heart. Pin in place. (Photo A)

3. Thread a needle with a length of embroidery thread, and tie a knot at the end. Sew around the edges of the smaller heart using a running stitch. Tie a knot on the back, and cut the thread. (Photo A)

4. Place the second rectangle on top of the first, with the right sides of the fabric facing each other. Trim across the top with pinking shears to prevent the edge from fraying. (Photo B)

5. Pin along the sides and the bottom. (Photo B)

6. Using a ¼-inch (6-mm) seam allowance, machine stitch the sides and bottom of the treat bag. When you get to a corner, make sure that the needle is down in the fabric before you lift the pressure foot to turn the fabric. After you turn the fabric, lower the pressure foot again and continue to sew. Trim the corners on a diagonal, being careful not to trim the stitches. This will create nice corners when you turn the bag right-side out.

7. Turn the bag right-side out. Fill with treats and tie with a ribbon to close. (Photo C)

A

B

C

A B C D

SAINT PATRICK'S DAY BOW TIE OR HAIR BOW

Don't get caught not wearing green! Make a bow tie or hair bow to wear on Saint Patrick's Day. If you're feeling really festive, make both! There's no such thing as too much green on Saint Patrick's Day.

sewing level: 1

Bow Tie templates (page 181)

Scissors

1 (9 x 3-inch [23 x 8-cm]) rectangle of green felt

Pin

Needle

Embroidery thread

1 (14-inch [36-cm]) piece of ¼-inch (6-mm)-wide elastic

Hot glue and glue gun (optional)

Metal hair clip (optional)

1. Using the cutting templates, create your patterns. Cut out 2 bow pieces and 1 small square of felt.

2. Pin the 2 bow pieces together. Thread a needle with a long length of embroidery thread, and tie a knot at the end. Sew around the edges using a running stitch. Tie a knot on the back, and cut the thread. (Photo A)

3. Overlap the ends of the elastic a ½ inch (13 mm). Secure with 2 stitches using your needle and embroidery thread. (Photo B)

4. Stitch the elastic in the center, on the back of the bow, with a few stitches. Tie a knot and cut the thread. (Photo C)

5. Attach the small square of felt to the front of the bow by stitching a large X. To do this, start from the back and stitch 1 large stitch diagonally, then another stitch diagonally on the opposite side. Tie a knot and cut the thread. (Photo D)

6. To make a hair clip, ask an adult to help you hot-glue the bow onto a metal hair clip instead of using elastic.

BUNNY BAG

Make a bunny bag to hold jelly beans at Easter time! You can even fill it with pillow stuffing for a cozy little friend to snuggle with.

sewing level: 2

1 (1 x 1-inch [2.5 x 2.5-cm]) square of scrap felt for the bunny face

Scissors

2 (4 x 8-inch [10 x 20-cm]) rectangles of felt

Needle

Embroidery thread

Pins

Sewing machine

Thread

Clear elastic hair band

1. Cut a small circle out of the scrap piece of felt (½ to 1 inch [13 to 25 mm]) for the bunny face. Place the circle 2½ inches (6 cm) from the bottom of 1 of the rectangles of felt. (Photo A)

2. Thread a needle with a length of embroidery thread, and tie a knot at the end. Make 3 stitches using embroidery thread to make a Y shape on the circle. This will create the bunny nose and mouth and stitch the circle of felt to the fabric at the same time! Tie a knot on the back, and cut the thread. (Photo A)

3. Change thread color and stitch 2 small X shapes for the eyes. Tie a knot on the back, and cut the thread. (Photo A)

4. Place the other rectangle of felt on your work surface. Place the one with the bunny face on top, looking at you, and line up the edges. Pin the sides and the bottom to keep everything in place. (Photo B)

5. Sew around the sides and bottom (leaving the top open) using the pressure foot on your sewing machine as a guide. Cut along the edge of the fabric with your scissors so that it is close to the seam that you just sewed. This will make a nice, clean-looking edge. (Photo C)

6. Measure 2½ inches (6 cm) from the top and mark this measurement with a pin. Use scissors to make a cut starting at the top and ending when you get to the pin. This will create two bunny ears! (Photo C)

7. Fill your bag with jelly beans or anything you'd like.

8. Tie the clear elastic hair band just below the ears to secure.

SHOOTING STAR T-SHIRT

Do you have a favorite Memorial Day or Fourth of July tradition? Maybe a parade in your town, a family barbecue or a fireworks show? This shooting star t-shirt is perfect to wear on any patriotic holiday!

sewing level: 3

1 (6-inch [15-cm]) square of fusible bonding (see note)

1 (6-inch [15-cm]) square of red cotton fabric

Iron

Ironing board

Star template (page 169)

Pencil or pen

Scissors

3 (6-inch [15-cm]) pieces of ½-inch (13-mm)-wide ricrac or ribbon

Pins

Plain t-shirt

Sewing machine

Thread

1. Ask an adult to help you iron the piece of fusible bonding web to the back of the red fabric, following the package instructions.

2. Using the cutting template, create a star pattern. Trace the star onto the back of the red fabric. Cut out the star. Peel the backing paper off the fabric. (Photo A)

3. Decide where you'd like the star and ricrac pieces on your shirt. Overlap the ends of the ricrac and add a few pins to keep the ricrac in place. Set the star to the side.

4. Machine stitch the ricrac onto your shirt. Sew straight through the middle of the ricrac from one end to the other. Repeat for the other 2 pieces of ricrac. Trim the threads. (Photo B)

5. Place the star onto your shirt and ask an adult to help you iron it into place. (Photo B)

6. Switch the stitch on your sewing machine from a straight stitch to a zigzag stitch.

   Keep the right inner edge of the pressure foot against the edge of the fabric at all times while you sew. Start with the needle in your fabric and zigzag stitch slowly around the entire star.

   When sewing around the star points, lift the pressure foot, with the needle still in the fabric, and pivot the fabric to go around the corners. Keep sewing until you reach the starting point. Backstitch a couple of stitches or stitch in place to create a knot. (Photo C)

7. Trim away any loose threads. (Photo D)

NOTE

Fusible bonding web is a backing that you can iron to the back of fabric to make an applique. You can buy it in a package or by the yard, just like you would for fabric. Follow the instructions on your package when applying it to the back of your fabric.

FRANKEN-STEIN DOOR HANGER

You will love this too-cute-to-spook door hanger to display for Halloween! You can even use the template as a blank canvas for creating a door hanger for any holiday. The sky is the limit!

sewing level: 2

Frankenstein templates (page 167 and 169)

Scissors

2 (8½ x 11-inch [22 x 28-cm]) sheets of black felt

1 (6 x 5-inch [15 x 13-cm]) rectangle of green felt

1 (4 x 2-inch [10 x 5-cm]) rectangle of white felt

1 (5 x 3-inch [13 x 8-cm]) rectangle of grey felt

2 black buttons

Embroidery thread

Needle

Pins

Sewing machine

Thread

1. Using the cutting templates, create your patterns. Cut 2 door hanger shapes from the black felt, 1 face from the green felt, 2 eyes from the white felt, 2 bolts from the grey felt and 1 mouth from the black felt. You will also need 2 tiny strips of black felt for eyebrows. They are too small to cut out with a template, so just do your best!

2. Place the 2 white circles onto the green face. Attach these by sewing a black button over each one with embroidery thread. (Photo A)

3. Cut a length of embroidery thread, and tie a knot at one end. Thread a needle with the other end. Use a running stitch to sew on the mouth and eyebrows. Tie a knot on the back, and cut the thread. (Photo B)

4. Use the same thread to backstitch 3 stitches on a diagonal for Frankenstein's "stitches," followed by 2 stitches going horizontally through the first 3 stitches you made. Tie a knot on the back, and cut the thread. (Photo B)

5. Place 1 of the door hanger shapes on your work surface. Layer the second one on top, lining up the edges. Place the 2 bolt shapes toward the bottom, 1 on each side. (Photo C)

6. Place the face on top and add a few pins to keep everything together. (Photo D)

7. Machine stitch using a ¼-inch (6-mm) seam allowance around the outer edge, along the top of the face and around the circle in the center. When you get to a corner or sharp curve, make sure that the needle is down in the fabric before you lift the pressure foot to turn the fabric. After you turn the fabric, lower the pressure foot again and continue sewing. Trim the threads.

A

B

C

D

BLACK CAT BEANBAG

This spooky little guy is filled with beans, so he can sit up on his own for a cute Halloween decoration. You can make a few to use for a beanbag toss game!

sewing level: 1

Cat templates (page 159)

Scissors

1 (8½ x 11-inch [22 x 28-cm]) sheet of black felt for the cat

1 (4-inch [10-cm]) square of orange felt for the heart

Embroidery thread

Needle

Pin

2 small green buttons

¾ cup (140 g) dry beans

1. Using the cutting templates, create your patterns. Cut out 2 cat shapes and 1 heart.

2. Thread a needle with embroidery thread, and tie a knot at the end. You can use a contrasting thread color to make the stitches stand out if you'd like.

3. Pin the heart shape to the center of the cat and hand stitch into place using a running stitch. Stitch the 2 buttons on for the eyes. (Photo A)

4. Place the other cat shape on your work surface and lay the front cat shape on top. Add a couple of pins to keep everything in place while you stitch them together.

5. Thread a long length of embroidery thread through a needle, and tie a knot at the end.

6. Using a whipstitch, start stitching on 1 of the ears and stitch all the way around until you get to the second ear. Use the space between the ears as an opening to fill with beans. (Photo B)

7. Spoon the dry beans into the opening. When it's as full as you'd like, finish up all of the stitching. Tie a knot and trim the thread. (Photo C)

PUMPKIN HOOP ART

Let's make a pumpkin wall hanging to display during the fall, especially at Thanksgiving! You can use this technique to make a wall hanging for any season by coming up with your own shape and changing the fabric. Try making a heart for Valentine's Day or a stocking for Christmas.

sewing level: 1

1 (4-inch [10-cm]) embroidery hoop

1 (5-inch [13-cm]) square of fabric for the background

Scissors

Pumpkin template (page 169)

1 (4 x 3-inch [10 x 8-cm]) rectangle of orange felt

Pin

Needle

Embroidery thread

1 (14-inch [36-cm]) piece of ½-inch (13-mm)-wide green ribbon

1. An embroidery hoop comes in 2 sections: the outside hoop and the inside hoop. To separate the two, twist the knob on the top and it will loosen the outside hoop. (Photo A)

2. Lay the background fabric over the inside hoop and then place the outside hoop on top. Push down on the outside hoop and it will sandwich the fabric in between both hoops, creating a tight fabric surface. Tighten the knob at the top. (Photo B)

3. Using scissors, cut off excess fabric all the way around the hoop.

4. Using the cutting template, create your pattern. Cut 1 pumpkin out of felt.

5. Pin it to the center of the hoop. (Photo C)

6. Thread a needle with a long piece of green embroidery thread. Tie a knot at the end.

7. Stitch all the way around the pumpkin and tie a knot in the back. Trim the thread. (Photo D)

8. Use the ribbon to tie a bow around the knob on the hoop, then hang it on the wall!

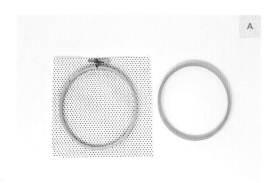

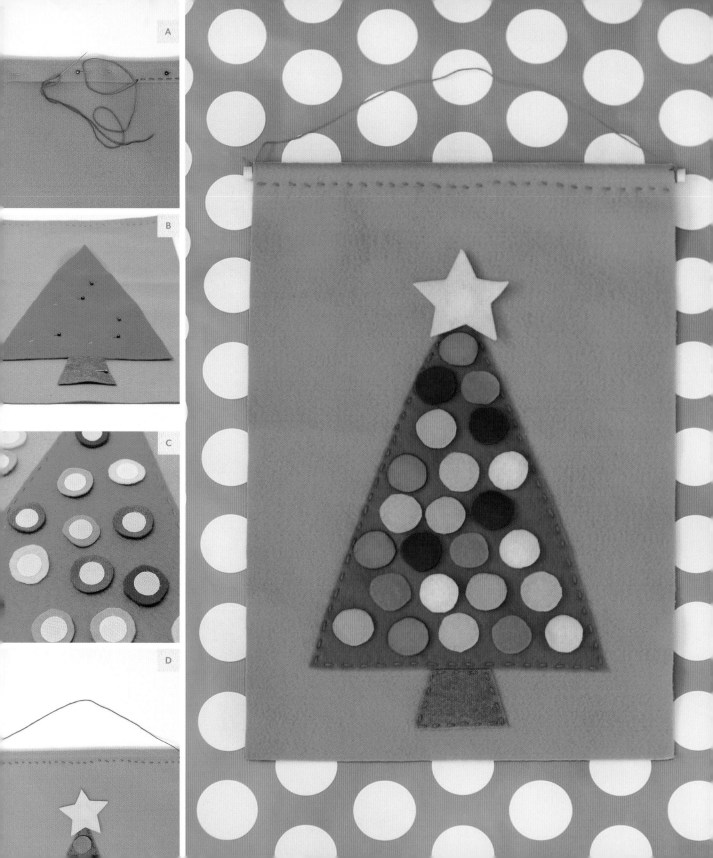

CHRISTMAS TREE ADVENT CALENDAR

Count down the days until Christmas with this colorful advent calendar! Starting on December 1st, add one ornament every day until Christmas Day, when you finally get to add the star to your tree!

sewing level: 1

Christmas Tree templates (page 153)

Scissors

1 (8½ x 11-inch [22 x 28-cm]) sheet of green felt for the tree

1 (3 x 3-inch [8 x 8-cm]) square of brown felt for the tree trunk

1 (4 x 4-inch [10 x 10-cm]) square of yellow felt for the star

6 (3 x 3-inch [8 x 8-cm]) squares of felt in a variety of colors for ornaments

1 (12 x 18-inch [31 x 46-cm]) sheet of blue felt for the background

Pins

Needle

Embroidery thread in a variety of colors

25 stick-on Velcro dots (see note)

1 (13 x ¼-inch [33-cm x 6-mm]) wood dowel

1. Using the cutting templates, create your patterns. Cut out 1 tree, 1 tree trunk, 1 star and 24 ornaments. This is a great project for using up felt scraps. You can cut 4 ornaments from each color of felt or any combination you'd like as long as you end up with 24.

Here's a tip for cutting the ornaments: Cut an ornament using the paper template, then use that felt ornament as a template for the other 23 remaining ornaments. Felt sticks to itself and won't slide around as much as a paper pattern.

2. Fold the top edge of your background sheet of felt down 1 inch (2.5 cm). Add a few pins to keep it in place. Thread a needle with matching embroidery thread and stitch across the bottom using a running stitch. Tie a knot in the thread and cut. (Photo A)

3. Arrange the tree and tree trunk on the felt background, making sure to leave room at the top for a star. Place pins all around to keep the felt in place. (Photo B)

4. Thread a needle with matching thread and stitch the tree trunk to the background. Tie a knot on the back and trim the thread.

5. Thread a needle with matching thread and stitch the tree to the background. Tie a knot on the back and trim the thread.

6. Place the scratchy sides of the Velcro stick-on dots onto the backs of the star and ornaments. (Photo C)

7. Slide a dowel through the top. Tie a long piece of 6-strand embroidery thread to each side. (Photo D)

8. Store the star and ornaments in a plastic baggie to keep them from getting lost so that you can use this for years to come.

NOTE

Velcro comes in two pieces: a soft side and a scratchy side. For this project, we are only using the scratchy side.

SNOWFLAKE ORNAMENT

Make a snowflake ornament to decorate your home this winter. You can use it to decorate a Christmas tree or even hang it from a doorknob!

sewing level: 2

2 (5-inch [13-cm]) circles of felt

Scissors

Needle

Embroidery thread

1 (6-inch [15-cm]) length of string or ribbon

Pins

Sewing machine

Thread

1. You can use a compass, a cereal bowl or any other round object to create a cutting template for your ornament.

2. Thread a needle with a long piece of embroidery thread. Tie a knot at one end. Poke the needle through the back of 1 of the circles in the center. Pull until the knot hits the back of the felt.

3. Starting from the center, use a backstitch and make 4 stitches going up, then go back to the center and make 4 stitches going down. It should be a solid line with 8 stitches. (Photo A)

   Do not tie a knot and cut your thread each time you start stitching in a different direction. Just keep stitching! The back of the circle will look like a mess of thread, but that's okay! We are going to cover it with the other circle of felt later.

4. Starting at the center once more, make 4 stitches going to the right, then go back to the center and make 4 stitches going to the left. It should look like a + sign. (Photo A)

5. Stitch 3 stitches going on a diagonal in between the 4 lines of stitches that you just completed. You should have 8 lines of stitching at this point. (Photo B)

6. Stitch a small stitch on each side of the top 2 stitches on all 8 lines. Tie a knot on the back, and cut the thread. (Photo C)

7. Cut a 6-inch (15-cm) piece of string and tie a knot in the end. Lay the back piece of felt on your work surface and place the string on top. Lay the front circle with the snowflake on top, sandwiching the string in between the layers. (Photo D)

8. Place a few pins around the edges. Place 1 pin on top of the string to keep everything together while you sew. (Photo D)

9. Machine stitch around the edge of the fabric using a ¼-inch (6-mm) seam allowance. Sewing around curves can be tricky. Go slow and adjust the fabric and pressure foot as needed. Trim the threads.

A

B

C

D

MINI CHRISTMAS STOCKING

This stocking is just the right size to tuck in a few small gifts or treats! Make one to decorate your home this holiday season or as a cool gift for a friend or family member.

sewing level: 3

Stocking template (page 175)

Scissors

¼ yard (0.23 m) of cotton fabric for the stocking

2 (5¼ x 2½-inch [13 x 6-cm]) pieces of felt for the stocking cuff

Pins

Sewing machine

Thread

Iron

Ironing board

1 (6-inch [15-cm]) piece of ½-inch (13-mm)-wide ribbon

1. Using the cutting template, create your pattern. Cut out 2 stocking pieces from your main fabric.

2. Place the stocking cutouts on your work surface with the right sides of the fabric facing you. Pin a cuff piece to the top of each stocking cutout. (Photo A)

3. Using the pressure foot on your sewing machine as a guide, sew the cuff piece to the top of each stocking piece. Trim the threads.

4. Open the seam so that the felt section is on top of the stocking, and ask an adult to help you iron the seams flat.

5. With the right sides of the fabric facing each other, pin the stocking front and back cutouts together. Place pins every couple of inches around the sides of the stocking. Stitch around the sides. Trim the threads. (Photo B)

6. Trim the curves close to the seam. This is a great trick for having nice, round edges when you turn your stocking right-side out. To do so, make cuts every ½ inch (13 mm) along the curves, but don't trim the stitching. (Photo C)

7. Turn the stocking right-side out and iron your project to smooth out everything.

8. Fold a piece of ribbon in half and pin to the top of the side seam. Sew across the ribbon, then sew again in reverse over the ribbon to reinforce the stitching. Trim the threads. (Photo D)

NOTE
You can create a larger stocking by enlarging the cutting template to the desired size!

GINGER-BREAD MAN SOFTIE

A darling gingerbread man that looks good enough to eat. Want to make a gingerbread girl? Turn that little bow tie into a hair bow! Get creative with buttons, ribbon or ricrac to create a one-of-a-kind cookie! You can set him on a shelf or on your bed for the whole month of December as a cute Christmas decoration!

sewing level: 2

Gingerbread Man templates (page 171)

Scissors

2 (8½ x 11-inch [22 x 28-cm]) sheets of brown felt for the gingerbread man

1 (2 x 2-inch [5 x 5-cm]) square of red felt for the bow tie

Buttons

1 (12-inch [31-cm]) piece of trim (ricrac or ribbon)

Needle

Embroidery thread

Pins

Sewing machine

Thread

1 small handful of pillow stuffing

Pencil

1. Using the cutting templates, create your patterns. Cut out 2 gingerbread-man shapes and 1 bow tie out of felt.

2. Arrange the buttons and trim to create a face and other details onto 1 of the gingerbread-man cutouts. Move things around until it looks just right. (Photo A)

3. Thread a needle with a length of embroidery thread, and tie a knot at the end.

4. Hand stitch the trim onto the front of the gingerbread man using a running stitch. Pin the trim on, if necessary, to keep it in place while you stitch. (Photo B)

5. Attach the bow tie to the gingerbread man by stitching a small button onto the center of the tie. (Photo B)

6. Sew the rest of the buttons on and use a backstitch to sew a mouth onto your gingerbread man.

7. Stack the top gingerbread-man cutout over the bottom gingerbread-man cutout, and add pins along the edge. Using plenty of pins will keep everything together while sewing around all of the curves on the gingerbread man. Mark a section under one of the arms with double pins. Leave this area open when you sew. You will use this opening to stuff the gingerbread man later. (Photo C)

8. Starting at one set of double pins, machine stitch the edge of the fabric using a ¼-inch (6-mm) seam allowance until you reach the second set of double pins. Take your time and go slowly around the curves. Adjust the position of the fabric when going around a sharp curve by keeping the needle in the fabric and raising the pressure foot. Pivot the fabric to its new position, lower the pressure foot and continue sewing. Trim the threads.

9. Add a small amount of stuffing to the gingerbread man. Begin with the head, then add a bit to the arms, legs and ending in the tummy area.

10. Use a pencil (eraser end) to help push stuffing where it needs to go. Pin the opening together and machine stitch to close. Trim the threads. (Photo D)

11. After sewing, you can trim close to the stitching for a cleaner edge.

RAINBOW POM-POM GARLAND

Make a fun and colorful pom-pom garland to hang in your bedroom or at a birthday party! This is a great beginner sewing project, and it comes together in just minutes. Use seasonal colors for holidays throughout the year if you like. You'll find yourself making them for every occasion!

sewing level: 1

42 inches (107 cm) white embroidery thread

Needle

1-inch (2.5-cm) pom-poms in a variety of colors

1. Tie a double knot 1 inch (2.5 cm) from the end of the thread.

2. Thread a needle with the embroidery thread and begin pushing the needle through the center of each pom-pom. Pull the pom-pom to the end of the thread and continue stringing them one by one. You can have the pom-poms touching or leave a small space between each one. (Photo A)

3. Continue adding pom-poms until you only have 1 inch (2.5 cm) of thread left. Tie another double knot in the thread. (Photo B)

PIN-TASTIC PROJECTS FOR YOUR BACKPACK

×××××××

There are probably days where you feel like you spend as much time at school as you do at home. If that's the case, you might as well feel organized and stylish while doing it! From Mini Journals (page 150) and Pocket Notebook Covers (page 141) to a Travel Tissue Pouch (page 149) and Lip Balm Key Chain (page 146), this chapter is loaded with projects for your backpack!

A

B

C

D

PENCIL POUCH

Keep pencils from getting lost in your backpack—with a pencil pouch! The top folds over and secures with a piece of Velcro to keep everything nice and secure.

sewing level: 1

1 (4 x 7½-inch [10 x 19-cm]) rectangle of felt

1 (4 x 10½-inch [10 x 27-cm]) rectangle of felt

Scissors

Pins

Needle

Embroidery thread

Measuring tape

Button

1 Velcro sticky dot

1. Place the short rectangle on top of the tall rectangle with the right side of the fabric facing out, making sure that the bottom and side edges line up. Place a few pins along the edges to keep everything in place. (Photo A)

One of the rectangle pieces is taller than the other. You will have an extra couple of inches sticking out on top. This will be the flap that folds over to keep the pencils from falling out.

2. Thread a needle with embroidery thread, and tie a knot at one end. Whipstitch the 2 pieces together along the sides and bottom. When you've finished the last stitch, tie a knot and trim the thread.

3. Fold the top flap down 2 inches (5 cm). (Photo B)

4. Cut a long length of thread. Thread a needle, and tie a knot at the end. Stitch a button along the bottom of the flap, in the center. (Photo C)

5. Open the flap and add one side of the sticky Velcro dot over the button stitches. Add the second dot on top of the first dot, with the sticky side facing you, then close the tab. Press firmly. This will line up the second dot perfectly onto the felt. (Photo D)

Open the flap and add your pencils to your new pencil pouch!

BAG TAG

Going on a trip for summer vacation? Make a luggage tag to keep track of your suitcase! Add your name and any other information you'd like with fabric markers. You can even make a tag with your name on it or maybe draw some doodles on it for your school backpack!

sewing level: 3

2 (3 x 5-inch [8 x 13-cm]) pieces of felt

1 (2 x 1½-inch [5 x 4-cm]) piece of paper for a cutting template

Scissors

1 (3 x 5-inch [8 x 13-cm]) piece of white cotton fabric

Fabric markers

1 (8-inch [20-cm]) piece of elastic cording (see note)

Pins

Sewing machine

Thread

1. Fold 1 of the felt rectangles in half. Place the small paper cutting template on the fold and trim around the 3 sides. This will create a window in your luggage tag so that you can see the white fabric behind it. (Photo A)

2. Decorate the center of the white rectangle with fabric markers. (Photo B)

3. Place the other large rectangle on your work surface. Add the white rectangle and then the rectangle with the window cutout. Make sure that all of the edges line up.

4. Fold your elastic cording in half and tie a knot on the end. (Photo C)

5. Slide the elastic cording in between the top 2 layers of your felt and cotton fabric. Add a pin on each side of the luggage tag to keep everything in place. (Photo D)

6. Using a sewing machine, stitch around all 4 of the sides using a ¼-inch (6-mm) seam allowance. When you get to a corner, make sure that the needle is down in the fabric before you lift the pressure foot to turn the fabric. After you turn the fabric, lower the pressure foot and continue sewing. Trim the threads.

NOTE
Elastic cording is thin and very stretchy elastic. You can find it at the craft store next to other types of elastic.

A

B

C

D

POCKET NOTEBOOK COVER

Make a colorful cover for a composition notebook! It even has a pocket to store pictures, stationery or stickers.

sewing level: 3

1 (25½ x 4-inch [65 x 10-cm]) rectangle for the pocket

Measuring tape

Iron

Ironing board

Sewing machine

Thread

Scissors

2 (25½ x 10½-inch [65 x 27-cm]) rectangles of fabric for the cover

Pins

1. Fold 1 of the long edges over ½ inch (13 mm) on the pocket piece. Ask an adult to help you iron the fold flat. Fold over ½ inch (13 mm) one more time. Iron the fold. You should now have a nice, clean edge on your fabric with a double fold. Sew through the center of the fold using a ¼-inch (6-mm) seam allowance. Trim the threads.

2. Lay 1 of the large rectangles of fabric on your work surface with the right-side of the fabric facing you. Place the pocket on top with the right side of the fabric facing you, and lining up the bottom edges. (Photo A)

3. Place the other large rectangle on top with the right side of the fabric facing down. Pin along the edges. Leave an opening to turn the cover right-side out. It sometimes helps to place 2 pins on each side of the opening. This will help you remember to stop sewing when you get to the double pins. (Photo B)

4. Start sewing at one set of double pins. Use the sewing machine pressure foot as a guide, keeping your fabric lined up with it as you sew. When you reach a corner, make sure that the needle is in the fabric. Lift the pressure foot, adjust the direction of the fabric and lower the pressure foot once more. Continue to sew until you reach the second set of double pins. Trim the threads.

5. After sewing all sides, carefully trim a small triangle off each corner for a neater finish when you turn the cover right-side out. Make sure not to cut too closely to your seam.

6. Turn the cover right-side out. Iron the edges nice and flat. Fold the edges of the opening over and pin in place. You're almost done! Now it's time to finish the side pockets for the notebook to slide into. (Photo C)

7. Fold the sides of the cover in 4½ inches (11 cm). This will create pockets on the side for the notebook to slide into. Place a pin on the top and bottom of each side pocket. (Photo D)

8. Topstitch a ¼-inch (6-mm) seam allowance around the entire edge of the notebook cover, stitching the opening closed and stitching along the top and bottom of each side pocket as you go. Trim the threads.

9. Slide the front and back cover of your notebook into the side flaps.

This notebook cover will fit a standard 7½ x 10-inch (19 x 25-cm) composition notebook.

CUPCAKE KEY CHAIN

Always know where your key is with this colorful cupcake key chain. It also makes a cute accessory for your backpack!

sewing level: 1

Cupcake templates (page 163)

Scissors

1 (8 x 4-inch [20 x 10-cm]) rectangle of felt for the cupcake

1 (4 x 3-inch [10 x 8-cm]) rectangle of felt for the frosting

1 (2 x 1-inch [5 x 2.5-cm]) rectangle for the loop

Embroidery thread in a variety of colors

Needle

Pins

1-inch (2.5-cm) key ring

1. Using the cutting templates, create your patterns. Cut out 2 cupcake shapes, 1 frosting shape and 1 small rectangle in whatever color of felt you'd like for the keychain loop.

2. Cut a few lengths of embroidery thread in different colors. Use all 6 strands in each color of the thread so that your stitches are bold. Because your thread will be thicker than normal, you may want to ask an adult to help you thread your needle. Tie a knot at the end.

3. Randomly stitch sprinkles onto the frosting shape in a variety of colors. Only tie a knot on the back when you are ready to change thread colors. The back of your frosting will look like a mess, but that's okay! (Photo A)

4. Now we are going to layer the cupcake pieces. Place both cupcake shapes on your work surface, the top over the bottom one. Lay the frosting piece on top. Use a couple of pins to hold everything in place. (Photo B)

5. Loop the key ring onto the felt strip. Bring both ends of the strip together and place in between the 2 cupcake shape layers. Pin the felt strip into place. (Photo C)

6. Cut a length of embroidery thread and thread a needle. Tie a knot at the other end. Using a running stitch, sew around the entire edge of the fabric and along the edge where the frosting meets the cupcake liner. Tie a knot on the back and trim the thread. (Photo D)

A

B

C

D

PENGUIN BOOKMARK

Keep your place in a favorite book or your school day planner with a cute penguin bookmark! The penguin and the fish will stick out on either side of your book. A nice little welcome to you each time you sit down to read!

sewing level: 1

Penguin templates (page 165)

Scissors

1 (4 x 8-inch [10 x 20-cm]) rectangle of black felt for the body and wings

1 (4 x 4-inch [10 x 10-cm]) square of white felt for the face

1 (2 x 2-inch [5 x 5-cm]) of orange felt for the beak

1 (5 x 2-inch [13 x 5-cm]) rectangle of blue felt for the fish

Pins

Embroidery thread in coordinating colors

Needle

1 (12-inch [31-cm]) piece of ½-inch (13-mm)-wide ribbon

1. Using the cutting templates, create your patterns. Cut out 2 circles for the body, 1 face, 2 wings, 1 beak and 2 fish shapes.

2. Pin the face to 1 of the body pieces and stitch around the edge of the face with a running stitch and embroidery thread. Do not cut the thread yet. Using the same thread, stitch 2 Xs for the eyes. Tie a knot on the back, and cut the thread. Change thread colors and stitch the beak onto the face. (Photo A)

3. Place the other body piece on your work surface. Overlap the wings just a bit on each side. Overlap one end of the ribbon ½ inch (13 mm) over the bottom edge.

4. Place the other body piece, with the face, on top. Pin the wings and ribbon in place to keep everything together while you sew. Cut a length of embroidery thread and thread the needle with one end. Tie a knot at the other end. Stitch around the body with a running stitch. Tie a knot at the back, and cut the thread. (Photo B)

5. Sandwich the other side of the ribbon between the 2 fish shapes. Add a pin to hold everything in place. Cut a length of embroidery thread, and thread the needle with one end. Tie a knot at the other end. Stitch around the fish using a running stitch. Tie a knot at the back, and cut the thread. (Photo C)

LIP BALM KEY CHAIN

Keep your lip balm from getting lost in your backpack by putting it on a key chain! This key chain is made out of ribbon, so it's a quick and easy project that you can customize using any color of ribbon you'd like!

sewing level: 3

1 (11-inch [28-cm]) piece of 1½-inch (4-cm) grosgrain ribbon

1 (1¼-inch [3-cm]) key ring

Pin

Sewing machine

Thread

Scissors

Measuring tape

1. Insert the top of the ribbon through the center of the key ring.

2. Fold the ribbon down 3 inches (8 cm). Use a pin to hold it in place. (Photo A)

3. Machine stitch in place by stitching close to the edge. (Photo B)

4. Sew another seam ½ inch (13 mm) below the key ring. Trim the threads.

5. Create a finished edge on the bottom of the ribbon by folding it up ¼ inch (6 mm) and then repeating. Sew through the center of the double fold. Trim the threads. (Photo C)

6. Fold the bottom of the ribbon 2½ inches (6 cm). Place a pin in the center of the ribbon, holding the fold in place. This will create the pocket for the lip balm. (Photo D)

7. Stitch from the bottom of the fold to the top edge on each side using a ⅛-inch (3-mm) seam allowance. Trim the threads.

A

B

C

D

TRAVEL TISSUE POUCH

Make a small travel pouch of tissues to keep inside your backpack. You never know when you or a friend may need one!

sewing level: 1

1 (5½ x 6½-inch [14 x 17-cm]) rectangle of felt

Measuring tape

Pins

Embroidery thread

Needle

Button (optional)

Scissors

1. Place the felt on your work surface with the 5½-inch (14 cm) side on the bottom. Fold the edge up 1¾ inches (4 cm) and pin in place. (Photo A)

2. Fold the top edge down so that it overlaps the bottom about ¼ inch (6 mm). Pin in place. (Photo B)

3. If you'd like to add a decorative button, thread a length of embroidery thread through a needle, and tie a knot at the end. Stitch the button onto the top or bottom flap. (Photo B)

4. Thread a length of embroidery thread through a needle, and tie a knot at the end. Whipstitch 1 side with small stitches. Tie a knot and cut the thread. Repeat for the other side.

5. Tuck a small, travel-size pouch of tissues inside.

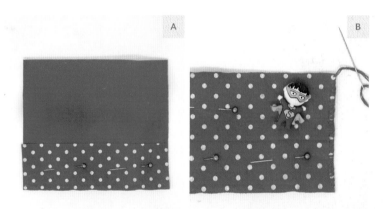

MINI JOURNALS

These mini journals come together in minutes and are just the right size to tuck inside a backpack. Write down your goals or take notes about your day!

sewing level: 1

3 (8½ x 11-inch [22 x 28-cm]) sheets of copy paper

Scissors or paper cutter

1 (9½ x 6-inch [24 x 15-cm]) piece of decorative scrapbooking paper (see note)

Pot holder

Pushpin

2 paper clips

Needle

Embroidery thread

1. Fold each piece of copy paper in half so that it measures 8½ x 5½ inches (22 x 14 cm). Cut each paper along the fold.

2. Fold the 6 pieces of copy paper in half. Fold the decorative scrapbooking paper in half. This piece will be the journal cover. Press firmly along the fold line with your fingers so that they lay nice and flat. (Photo A)

3. Open each paper and stack together with the decorative paper on the bottom and the copy papers on top. Make sure that the folds line up.

4. Lay your bundle of papers on top of a pot holder. Use the pushpin to poke holes every ½ inch (13 mm) or so along the fold of the copy paper. (Photo B)

5. Place a paper clip on each side of the fold to keep the papers together while you sew. (Photo C)

6. Thread a needle with a long piece of embroidery thread, tie a knot at the end and stitch along the fold. Work your way from the bottom to the top. Tie a knot when you reach the last hole and cut the thread. (Photo C)

7. Fold your mini journal in half.

NOTE
You can make two journal covers from one 12 x 12-inch (31 x 31-cm) sheet of scrapbook paper.

PROJECT TEMPLATES

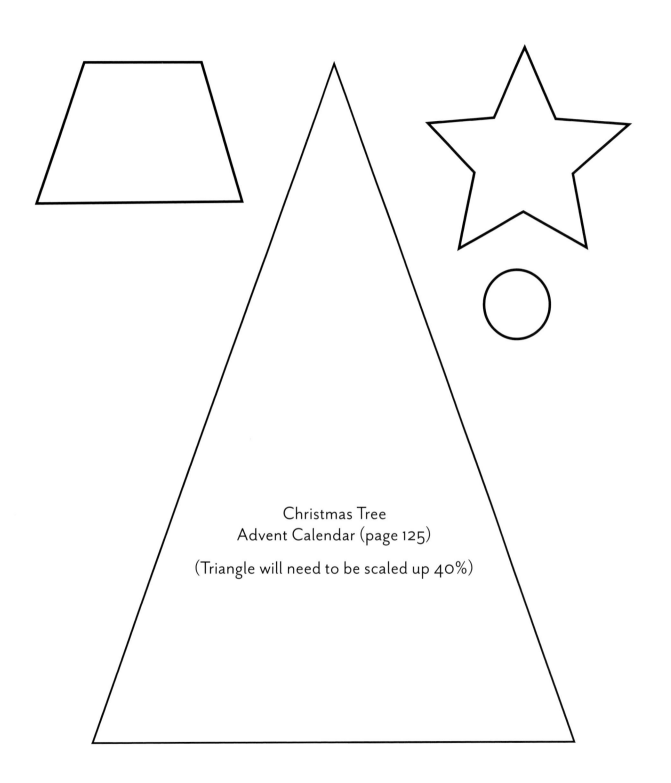

Christmas Tree
Advent Calendar (page 125)

(Triangle will need to be scaled up 40%)

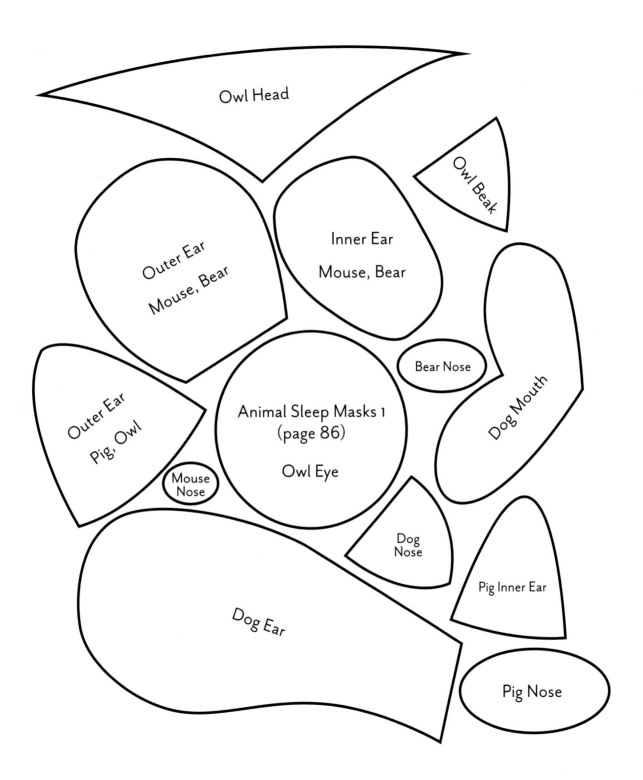

Owl Head

Owl Beak

Outer Ear
Mouse, Bear

Inner Ear
Mouse, Bear

Bear Nose

Dog Mouth

Outer Ear
Pig, Owl

Animal Sleep Masks 1
(page 86)

Owl Eye

Mouse
Nose

Dog
Nose

Pig Inner Ear

Dog Ear

Pig Nose

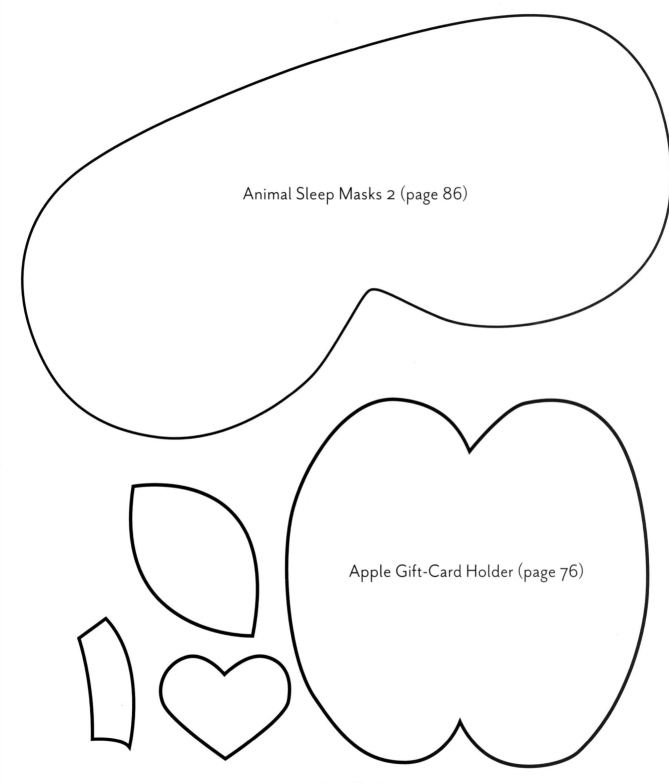

Animal Sleep Masks 2 (page 86)

Apple Gift-Card Holder (page 76)

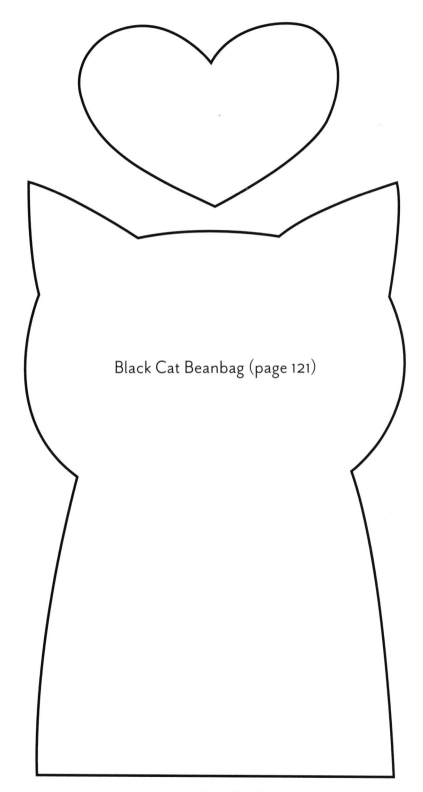

Black Cat Beanbag (page 121)

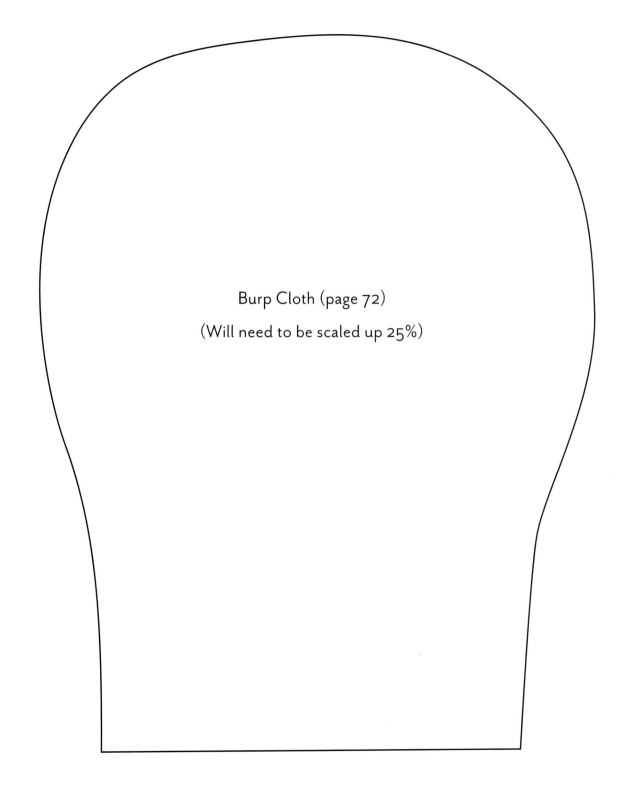

Burp Cloth (page 72)

(Will need to be scaled up 25%)

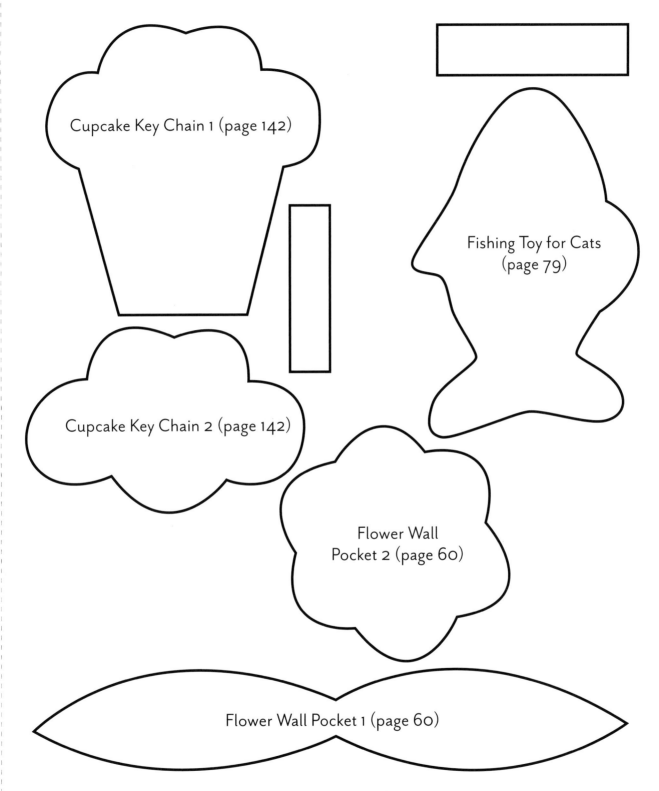

Cupcake Key Chain 1 (page 142)

Fishing Toy for Cats (page 79)

Cupcake Key Chain 2 (page 142)

Flower Wall Pocket 2 (page 60)

Flower Wall Pocket 1 (page 60)

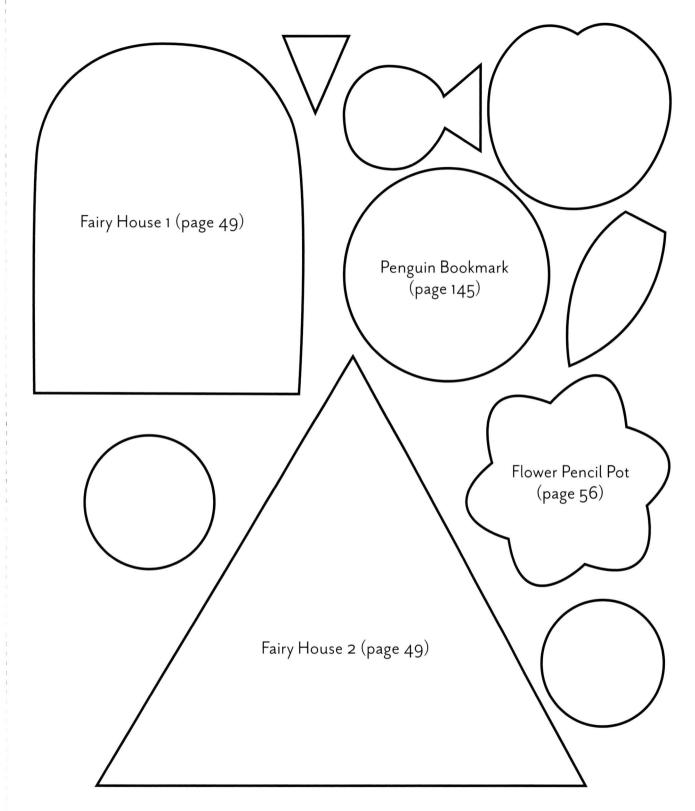

Fairy House 1 (page 49)

Penguin Bookmark
(page 145)

Flower Pencil Pot
(page 56)

Fairy House 2 (page 49)

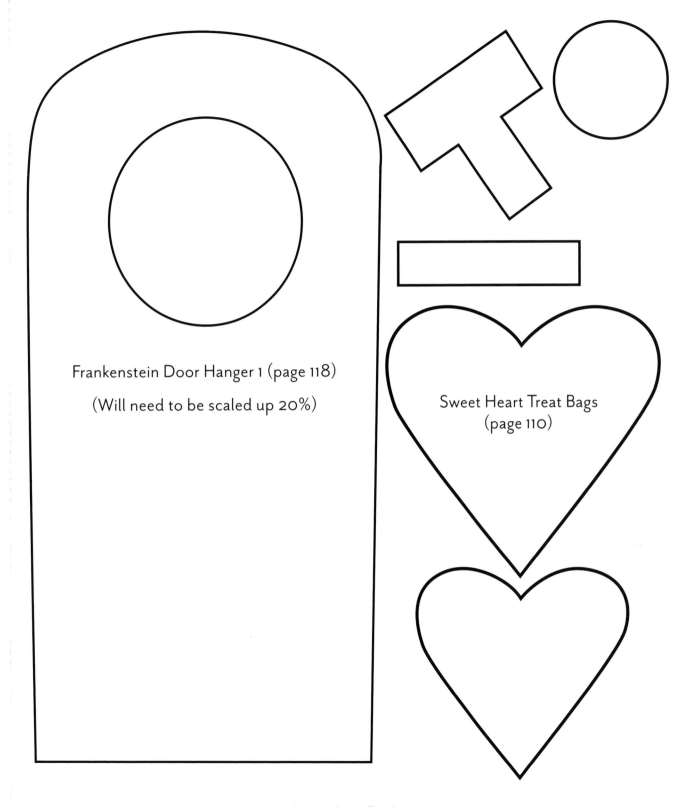

Frankenstein Door Hanger 1 (page 118)

(Will need to be scaled up 20%)

Sweet Heart Treat Bags
(page 110)

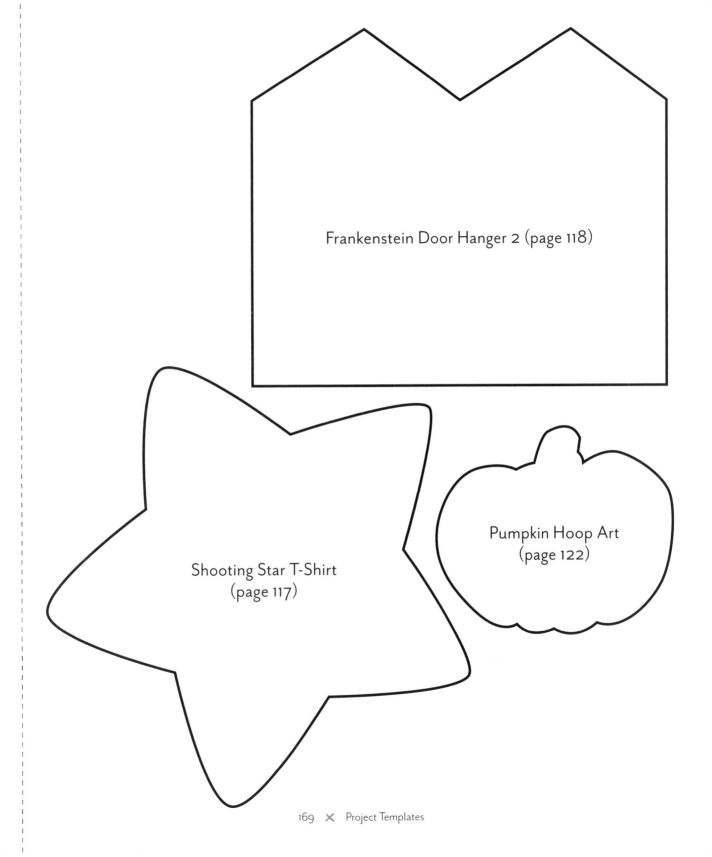

Frankenstein Door Hanger 2 (page 118)

Shooting Star T-Shirt
(page 117)

Pumpkin Hoop Art
(page 122)

Gingerbread Man Softie (page 130)

(Will need to be scaled up 20%)

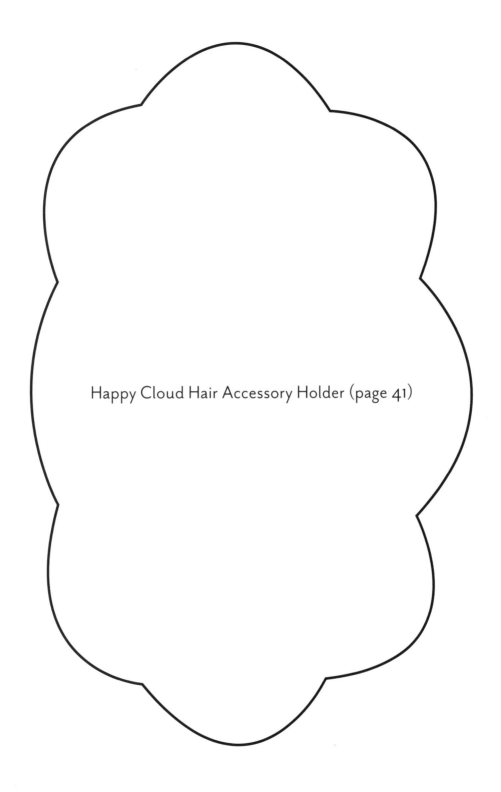

Happy Cloud Hair Accessory Holder (page 41)

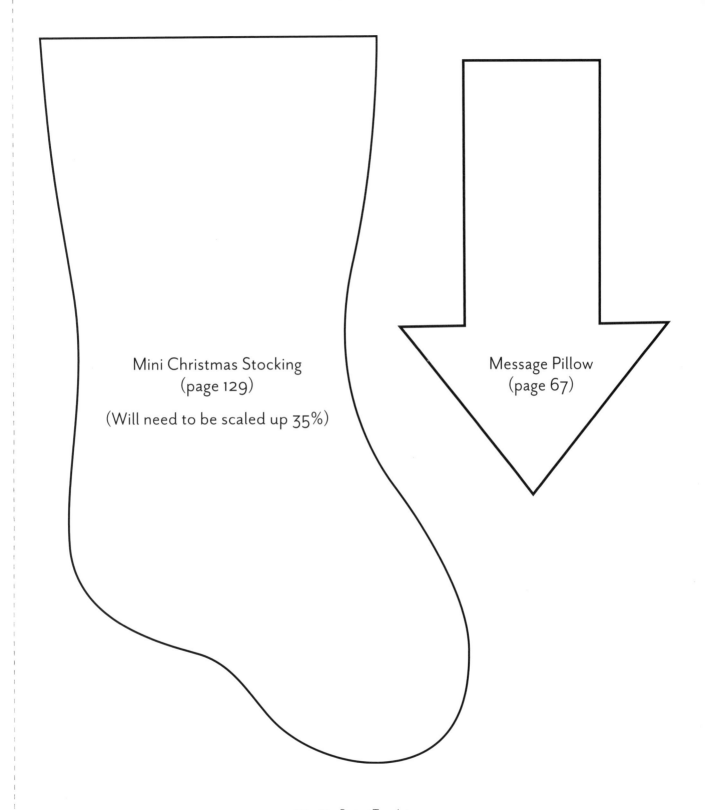

Mini Christmas Stocking
(page 129)

(Will need to be scaled up 35%)

Message Pillow
(page 67)

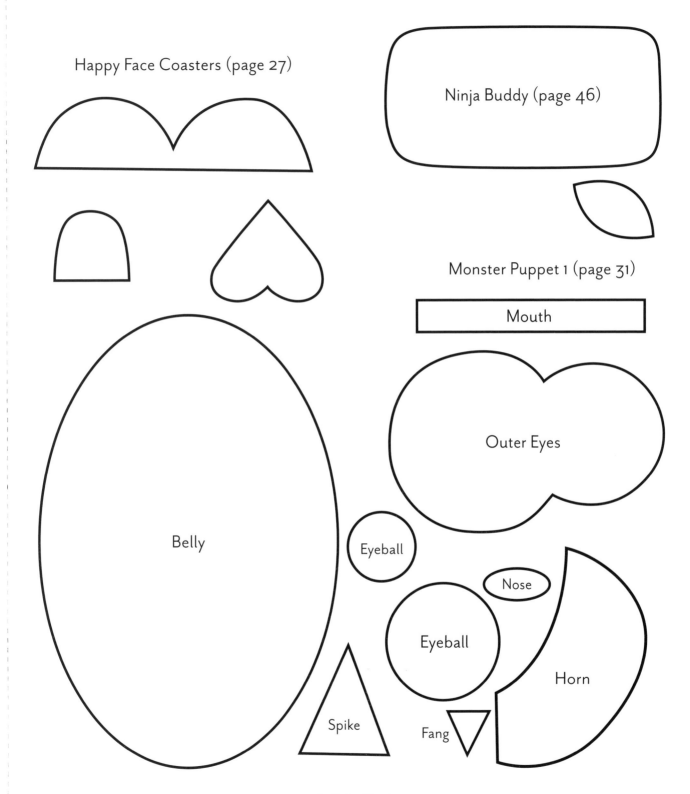

Happy Face Coasters (page 27)

Ninja Buddy (page 46)

Monster Puppet 1 (page 31)

Mouth

Outer Eyes

Belly

Eyeball

Nose

Eyeball

Horn

Spike

Fang

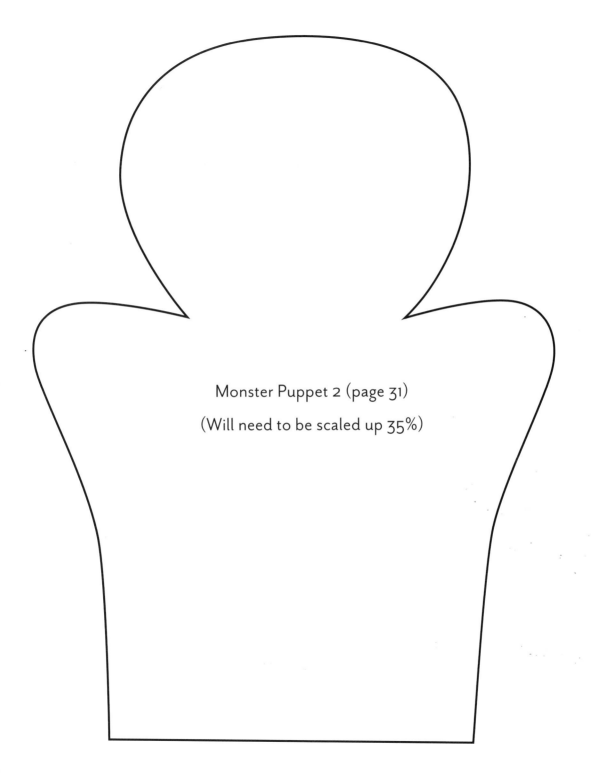

Monster Puppet 2 (page 31)

(Will need to be scaled up 35%)

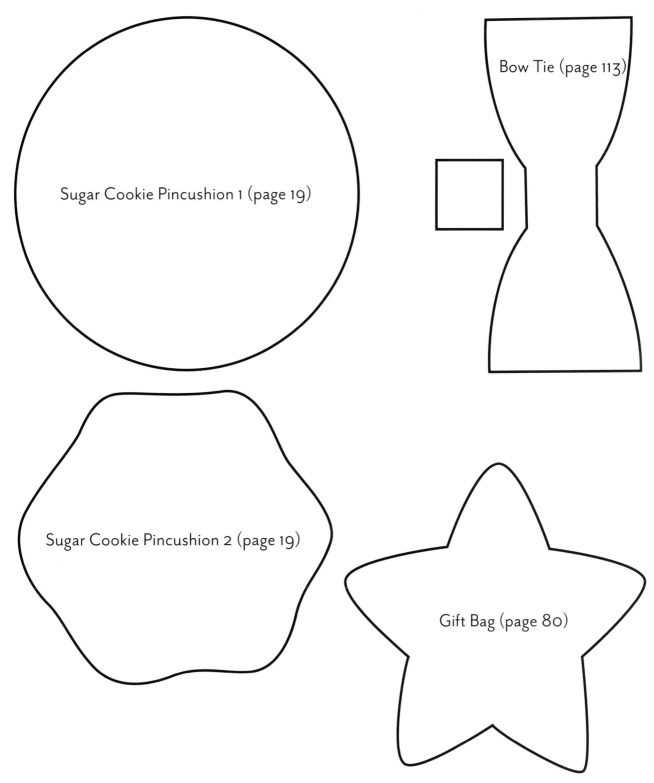

Sugar Cookie Pincushion 1 (page 19)

Bow Tie (page 113)

Sugar Cookie Pincushion 2 (page 19)

Gift Bag (page 80)

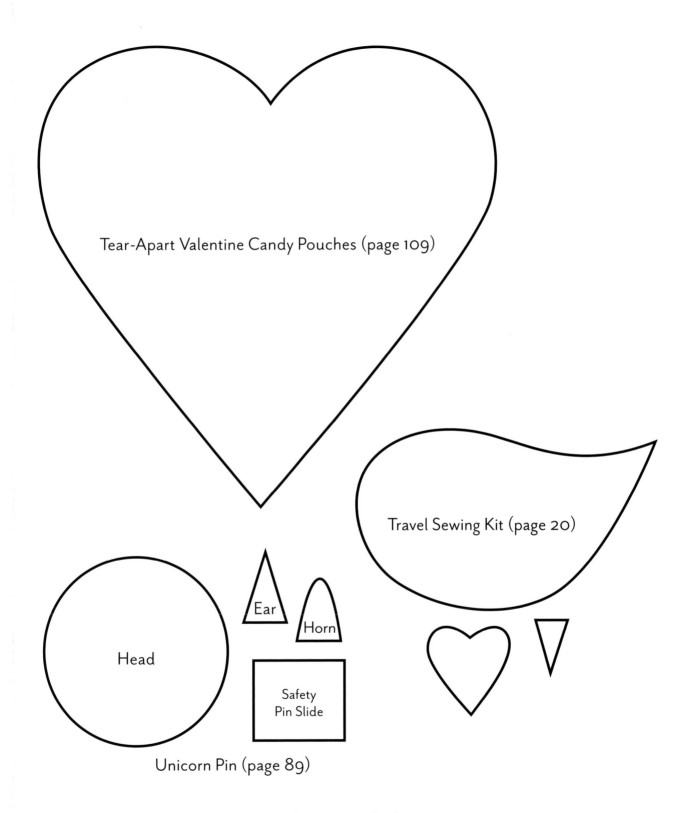

Tear-Apart Valentine Candy Pouches (page 109)

Travel Sewing Kit (page 20)

Ear

Horn

Head

Safety
Pin Slide

Unicorn Pin (page 89)

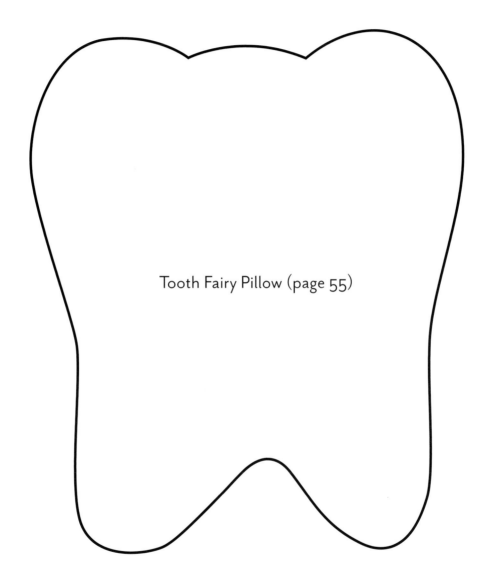

Tooth Fairy Pillow (page 55)

ACKNOWLEDGMENTS

Derrick, I will never forget coming home from work, only being married for a couple of months, and finding a brand-new sewing machine on the kitchen table with the note that said, "Make me something pretty." I hadn't sewn in quite some time and my skills were beginner, at best, but you knew that it was something that I enjoyed. Thank you for pulling a few of my sewing projects out of the trash during those first couple of years and encouraging me to try again when some of the frustration wore off. You are my biggest support, and I love this life that we have created together.

Dallin, Aaron, Kaylee, Ruby and Mac, I wrote this book for you. From the Ninja Buddies to the Animal Sleep Masks, your favorite colors, animals and hobbies were my inspiration. We've had so much fun crafting since you were toddlers, and I'm looking forward to making even more projects together!

Mom and Dad, thank you for buying Stacy and me that old sewing machine at a yard sale 28 years ago, and for letting us go through your craft supplies and make décor for our bedroom and gifts for others. I try to remember how much fun I had doing that when I see my girls making a mess of my craft room now.

To my editors, Elizabeth Seise and Sarah Monroe, you were a breath of fresh air throughout the entire process. Always answering my ridiculous amount of questions with patience, and putting my mind at ease. It was so exciting to see the book take shape, thanks to your guidance and input. To the design team, from the preliminary cover design to seeing the first chapter come together, it's as if you read my mind. The colors, the fonts, the entire feel of the book is as fun and cheerful as I had imagined! Thank you, Will Kiester and the entire Page Street Publishing team, for this tremendous opportunity.

To my followers who have become friends over at Gluesticks, thank you for your comments, ideas and support!

ABOUT THE AUTHOR

Brandy Nelson is the author of the blog Gluesticks and an avid DIY enthusiast. Her sewing tutorials, children's activities, recipes and printables have been featured in *All You* magazine, *Taste of Home*, Apartment Therapy, craftgawker and *FamilyFun* magazine. When given the choice between a good book and a sewing project, the fabric and scissors always win. Brandy enjoys traveling the country with her husband, five children and black Lab. They currently reside in the beautiful state of Virginia.

INDEX